BE SMART ABOUT SEX

Facts for Young People

Jean Fiedler and Hal Fiedler, Ph.D.

Drawings by Hal Fiedler

ENSLOW PUBLISHERS, INC.

Bloy St. & Ramsey Ave.
Box 777
Hillside, N.J. 07205
U.S.A.

P.O. Box 38
Aldershot
Hants GU12 6BP
U.K.

Library of Congress Cataloging-in-Publication Data
Fiedler, Jean.
    Be smart about sex: facts for young people/by Jean Fiedler and
Hal Fiedler.
      p. cm.
    Bibliography: p.
    Includes index.
    ISBN 0-89490-168-0
    1. Sex instruction for teenagers—United States—Miscellanea. 2. Sex instruction
for children—United States—Miscellanea.
    I. Fiedler, Hal. II. Title.
HQ35.F45 1990   89-7919
613.9'51—dc20   CIP

Printed in the United States of America

10 9 8 7 6 5 4 3 2

Contents

Acknowledgments

The authors want to thank the young people who have told of their experiences and whose questions have challenged us to learn what we could about responsible sexuality in these times.

We have used information obtained from Centers for Disease Control, United States Public Health Service, The Institute for Advanced Study of Human Sexuality, SIECUS, Planned Parenthood Federation of America, Gay Men's Health Crisis, San Francisco AIDS Foundation, San Francisco Public Library, Queens Borough Public Library, and the New York Public Library.

We are grateful to Dr. Wardell B. Pomeroy, Dr. Loretta Haroian, Dr. Eleanor Hamilton, The Rev. Dr. Ted McIlvenna, The Rev. Dr. Laird Sutton, and Dr. Clark Taylor for the philosophy and inspiration that motivated us to undertake this project.

1

Introduction

We live in a new age—the Age of AIDS. The outbreak of this deadly disease requires us to follow new guidelines regarding sex in our lives and to become alert to new risks in the use of drugs and alcohol.

Newspaper headlines call AIDS an epidemic. People are frightened because there is, as yet, no preventive. Nor is it likely that there will be a vaccine in the near future to protect us from AIDS.

Epidemic is a scary word. It means a disease that spreads rapidly and affects a large number of people. And AIDS *is* scary, but it is different from the epidemics of past centuries like cholera and smallpox in that people can remain safe from the dangers of AIDS just by changing behaviors and attitudes.

In changing times new questions come up and old ones are seen in a new light. Let's look at some of the questions that young people are asking.

"There are certain things I've never talked about to anyone. How do I find out what I want to know in this book?"
First, look through the Index at the back of the book for the topics that interest you, and then turn to the pages that are listed. If you are uncertain about the meaning of a word you may have heard or read, see the Words and Meanings section, page 116. You may not find all the answers to your questions on these pages, but on pages 114 and

115 we list Hotline phone numbers. If you call them, your questions should be answered expertly with up-to-the-minute information.

Readers have different needs. Each of you is at an individual stage of sexual development, and your interests are very different. The questions young people ask reflect these interests. This book tries to answer the questions that arise at different stages of development.

Some readers will find that there are chapters that deal with matters they know all about. Others will find that some of the chapters deal with subjects that do not interest them now and may or may not ever be important to them.

"What if I don't want to have sex?"

This guide will help you stick to your guns. It will make it easier for you to say clearly what you do not want as well as what you do want.

Fifteen-year-old Laurel wonders about the advice, "Say *no* to sex." She says: **"I can say 'no' to intercourse—that's far in the future for me anyway. But what else am I saying 'no' to? Does it mean saying 'no' to kissing or any kind of touching?"**
As you guessed, for some people, it does mean saying no to any kind of physical contact. Some religious leaders believe that physical contact before marriage is dangerous and wrong. Others hold the view that kissing and light petting are fine, but that you must say no to sexual intercourse. It may be helpful to ask your parents what "saying *no* to sex" means to them. And if you belong to a religious faith, talking to your minister, rabbi, or priest seems like a good idea too.

"I've been having sex for a while. Must I stop now because of AIDS?"

Stopping is one solution—the only completely safe one. But some young people have not been accepting the advice to put off sex. If you are continuing to have sexual intercourse, you do need new guidelines so that you can make responsible decisions and so that you can protect

6

both your life and your partner's. This book will provide these guidelines. See Chapter Six for a discussion of ways to reduce the health risks in sexual intercourse.

"I don't know what I want to do about sex. Will this book tell me what to do?"

There are many books that give advice on which sexual behaviors are

considered appropriate for young people. The intention of *Be Smart About Sex* is to provide new factual information that young people can use in making their own decisions. Sexual choices are made against a conflicting background of parental values, religious traditions, messages from the media, and local teenage customs. They are often difficult choices to make because some conflict is unavoidable. But having adequate information will help you arrive at better decisions.

"I'm getting too scared to read about AIDS. Can't they just put away those people who have it so we can be safe?"
Hysteria is in the air; it is all around us. It is fanned by inflammatory newspaper headlines and by unfounded rumors. It is this hysteria that makes us look for people to blame. Hysteria can become an even more dangerous epidemic than AIDS.

What you fear is the unknown. You must take the trouble to learn the real facts about AIDS—the specific ways that AIDS is spread and what you can do to protect your health. Your safety depends on acting responsibly, in your own best interests.

"How do I know what to believe and what not to believe?"
You can rely on the objective information that you will find in both school and public libraries. It is important to know the facts and to compare opposing viewpoints, so that you can stay levelheaded and not give in to hysteria.

* * *

In this Age of AIDS the rules for sexual behavior must be revised. But many readers are just beginning to feel sexual urges and are experiencing puzzling changes in their bodies and emotions. The next chapter will discuss these changes—the changes that take place during the first years of sexual development in the young woman and in the young man.

2

Changes in the Early Teen Years

"What's wrong with me? Why is my body acting weird?
There is nothing wrong. The body's reproductive system is waking up
to a kind of alarm clock in the brain. Sometime before the age of twelve
or so, there is an increase in the body's production of growth hormones. Hormones are chemical substances that are produced in the
body's glands. It is the accelerated production of sex hormones that is
responsible for beginning sexual development.

THE GIRLS SPEAK:

**"I'm taller than all the boys in my sixth-grade class. It seemed to
happen overnight. What can I do to stop growing?"**
The hormones cause a sudden spurt in growth. At first, most girls grow
faster than boys, and this unexpected change can make them feel
awkward. The boys feel strange about this height difference, too.

Roberta says she feels like a freak:
"My mother says I'm having my 'growth spurt,' but I think I'm
growing into a giant. I've always been kind of tall, but now I'm
taller than all the boys in the class and I'm even as tall as my teacher.
If I keep going at this rate, I'll be hitting the ceiling soon."

Everybody is different and no two people start their rapid growth stage at exactly the same age. But you *can* stop worrying—the sudden growth stops as naturally as it started!

Sue says:

"I've always been kind of shy and quiet, and I still am. But a few months ago my breasts started to swell, and now I can't walk through the halls without boys whistling at me. I haven't changed, but my breasts are giving guys the wrong message."

And her friend, Jane, adds:

"My best friend has a bust like a movie star. The boys call her sexy, but she hates it. I'm confused and I know she is too. What does sexy really mean?"

Sexy usually means arousing or sexually exciting. The boys who call her "sexy" are aroused by the sight of her large breasts. Of course she is not responsible for the development of her breasts. That tendency is inherited, like the color of hair and eyes.

Her body, unlike the boys' bodies, has not yet gotten the hormone signals that can cause *her* to feel sexual urges. So although she appears sexy to them, she does not *feel* sexy at all. This difference in developmental timing often causes misunderstanding between girls and boys.

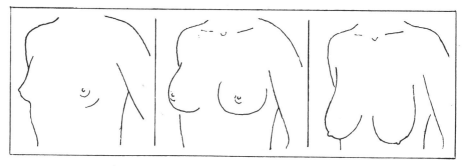

Women's breasts vary in size and shape. They develop at different ages. Some girls' breasts may start swelling when a girl is as young as eight and some much later. There is no universally ideal size or shape, though most cultures consider breasts beautiful.

Julie says: "My boobs have begun to swell, but one breast is larger than the other. I'm the only girl I know who has lopsided breasts. It's so embarrassing that I stuff my bra with cotton to make my boobs look the same size. Is something wrong with me?"

Nothing is wrong. These differences in breast size are common to most girls as the breasts develop; there is no cause for concern. Breasts usually seem to even out, but for some women one breast may remain slightly larger than the other. There is never any perfect symmetry in the human body.

BODY CHANGES OF EARLY TEEN YEARS

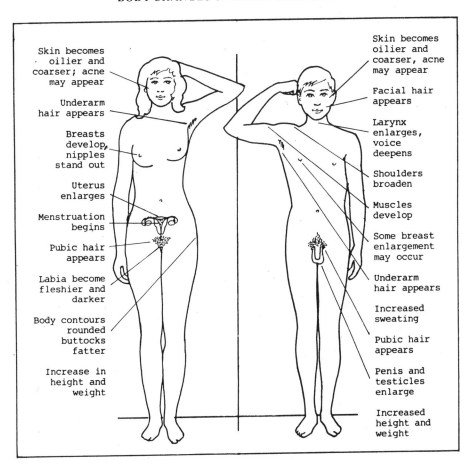

Skin becomes oilier and coarser; acne may appear

Underarm hair appears

Breasts develop, nipples stand out

Uterus enlarges

Menstruation begins

Pubic hair appears

Labia become fleshier and darker

Body contours rounded buttocks fatter

Increase in height and weight

Skin becomes oilier and coarser, acne may appear

Facial hair appears

Larynx enlarges, voice deepens

Shoulders broaden

Muscles develop

Some breast enlargement may occur

Underarm hair appears

Increased sweating

Pubic hair appears

Penis and testicles enlarge

Increased height and weight

Breast development comes in stages. The first change is usually a darkening of the area around the nipple (the areola). Second, the nipples get larger and begin to stand out more. (Some turn in instead of sticking out—these are called inverted nipples.) The third change is growth of the breast, and often one breast will start growing first, the other lagging behind.

"Why am I getting hair down there when I don't even have my period yet?"

One of the first signs of female sexual development is the growth of hair above the vulva (the external genitals) and then under the arms. It means that menstruation will probably start soon, too.

In some girls the first sign of puberty is the sudden "growth spurt"; in others it may be changes in body shape. Pubic hair may begin to appear on some girls as young as eight, while others may not develop pubic hair until they are sixteen or even older. Some women have sparse pubic hair growth; on others the growth is dense. Any pattern is normal.

Carla, concerned about getting her first period, says:

"When my girl friends started to get their periods, I was kind of glad I wasn't the first one. But now I'm fourteen—the only girl I know who hasn't begun to menstruate. I'm beginning to feel

STAGES OF PUBIC HAIR GROWTH

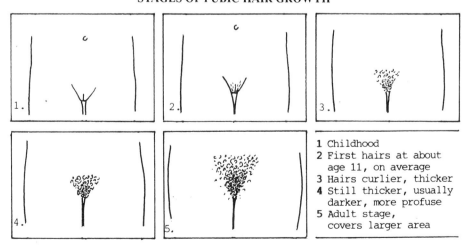

1 Childhood
2 First hairs at about age 11, on average
3 Hairs curlier, thicker
4 Still thicker, usually darker, more profuse
5 Adult stage, covers larger area

12

abnormal. My napkins have been lying in my drawer for two years now. I wonder if I'm ever going to get it."

Most girls want their development to be "in sync" with that of their friends, but there is no "right age" to start menstruation. Some girls start menstruation as early as nine, some as late as sixteen.

"I'm thirteen, and I just got my first period. Does that mean that I can now get pregnant?"

Yes, it does. Even if you are not at all interested in sex now, it is important for you to know all about your own body, including the reproductive system. And it is important for you to know all about the male reproductive system as well.

This is the time to learn the facts about conception—before you ever want to "have sex." Knowing the facts can help you avoid an unplanned pregnancy. Become informed now so that when you are mature enough for your first sexual experiences they can be pleasurable ones. The information you need may be found in Chapter Nine.

FEMALE EXTERNAL GENITALS

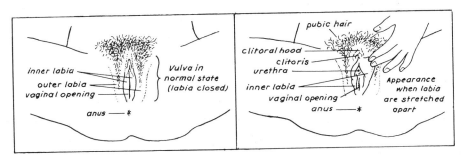

No two vulvas (external genitals) look exactly alike. The greatest variations are in appearance of the inner labia (lips), which are sometimes very large. The vaginal opening cannot be seen open except with a plastic speculum, used for examining the cervix.

The clitoris is the part most sensitive to stimulation. Most of it is deep in the body and responds to pressure. The small head of the clitoris (not always visible) is extremely sensitive and is easily irritated if it is stimulated too vigorously or without moisture.

Growth hormones that are helping your body to mature are also causing temporary changes that may be making you uncomfortable. Anna feels miserable about how her skin is reacting to her new hormone state.

"Just last year, my mother's friends would rave about my beautiful skin. But now when I look in the mirror, I feel like crying. Every day I seem to find a new pimple or blackhead. I can't imagine a guy ever wanting to kiss me."

"I hate the way I look. Am I always going to have pimples?"

That's unlikely. Sooner or later your pimples will disappear. You have plenty of company because so many other teens have skin problems, too. But there are things to do that may help.

The same hormones that are developing your body and giving it new curves are, unfortunately, making your skin oily and causing the eruption of pimples and blackheads.

To avoid scarring, it is best not to squeeze or pick at pimples or blackheads. What you *can* do is to wash your face two or three times a day. Ordinary soap or an antibacterial soap will help reduce the oiliness. After washing with warm water, rinse with cold water to help close the pores. It is a good idea to wash your hair often too.

But if you have severe acne, a doctor should be seen. There are some prescription medications that may help.

"I'm embarrassed sometimes when my pants get wet. Why does this happen to me?"

The wetness comes from vaginal lubrication. Now that your body is producing more sex hormones, your vagina will feel wet more often, and this often accompanies a sexy thought or feeling. Lubrication is a natural function that most women experience.

"Why do I get depressed a few days before my period?"

The emotional and physical discomforts that many young women experience in the week before their period seem to be due to hormonal changes.

Some girls feel blue and edgy, get headaches, cry easily, or flare up unpredictably. Some have cramps in the abdomen or experience lower back pain. These pains and upsets are annoying but nothing to worry about—they usually disappear a day or so after the period begins.

Brenda, who is fourteen, is trying to do something about her discomfort:
"I've become a regular Jekyll and Hyde. A few days before my period, I'm impossible—everything anybody says is wrong. My moods go up and down like a yo-yo. If my dad tries to tease me out of it, I either get mad or I begin to cry.

"My mother says, 'You'll feel better as soon as you get your period.' The crazy thing is—I always do—until the next month. I read in a magazine that giving up sugar, salt, and fried foods for a few days before you begin to menstruate may help. I'm going to try it!"

Cutting down on cola drinks, coffee, and tea is also a good idea

CUTAWAY DRAWINGS OF VAGINA AND UTERUS

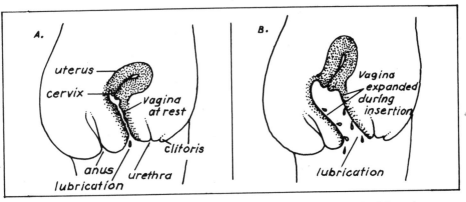

Vaginal lubrication is moisture that oozes through the mucous membrane walls of the vagina when some sexual stimulation (a thought or touch) has caused increased blood supply in the vaginal muscle tissue.

The vagina is normally closed, like a flattened tube, as shown in Diagram A. The elastic walls are easily pressed open, as in Diagram B, by the entering penis (or finger or examining instrument). During childbirth the vagina stretches much more to allow the baby to pass through.

15

because they all contain caffeine, which may be a particularly trouble-making substance during the premenstrual days. Wine and beer increase headache and cramping for some women. It's a good idea to get some kind of regular exercise and sufficient sleep.

"I don't understand what's happening to me. All of a sudden I'm self-conscious and shy around boys."

At your age a surge of hormones is causing body feelings and emotional reactions that are new and strange and uncomfortable. Your friends, both female and male, are going through similar changes.

Patty complains of her new awkwardness:

"I grew up with my brothers and their friends. At times I thought I was 'one of the boys.' Then a few months ago—right after I got my period for the first time—everything changed. I didn't want to play ball because then the boys would see my breasts jiggle.

"I began to feel shy and peculiar and when they kidded around, I found myself blushing. I miss my old friends and the way it was."

It would be easier for everybody if you and your friends all compared notes about what you are feeling instead of thinking that you are the only person in the world who is going through this difficult time. Talking to your friends about these changing feelings will lessen the self-consciousness and embarrassment.

The boys, too, feel awkward. It would be good to remember that the boys are equally self-conscious and, like you, are struggling to conceal it. That is why they seem to act so weirdly at times.

"When my friends are around, why is it that everything my parents say embarrasses me?"

Your friends are finding their own parents embarrassing and probably are hardly aware of yours. Although you may see your parents differently now, it is unlikely that they have suddenly changed—they are the same people with whom you were comfortable a short time ago.

Suddenly their shortcomings seem magnified because in this new growth phase teens tend to become supercritical of themselves and of the people closest to them. Holly says:

"I love my parents, but they seem to go out of their way to embarrass me. My mother tries to get 'buddy buddy' with my friends and even to talk the way we do. I could die when she uses a 'kid word.' All I can do is roll my eyes at my friends so at least they know I'm embarrassed. If I try to talk to her about it, she acts like I'm trying to hurt her.

"My dad likes to joke and still pinches my friends' cheeks the way he did when they were eight. Why can't they realize we're not little girls anymore and leave us alone!"

These uncomfortable feelings will pass in the normal course of events, but life will be easier right now if you can try to tolerate them.

THE BOYS SPEAK:

Boys have their problems with rapid growth, too. It feels strange when one part of the body (usually the feet or legs) suddenly enlarges, out of proportion to the rest of the parts.

Jerry laments:

"I've heard of guys my age getting taller, but who ever heard of a kid whose feet grew and left him behind? It seemed that overnight my feet began to grow and didn't know when to stop. The kids think it's a great joke to call me 'Big Foot.' Sometimes I wish I could disappear!"

Bruce says:

"Everybody is growing but me. When I go places with my friends, I look like their little brother tagging along. I made my mother take me to the doctor, but he was no help. All he said was, 'Be patient. You'll catch up.'"

And, like the girls, boys suddenly find their parents embarrassing. Louis adds his complaint:

"When I was a kid, I was sick a lot with allergies and colds, and my mother can't seem to remember I'm not that little kid anymore. When I'm going out with the guys and she reminds me to take a sweater, I feel like I'm five years old. As soon as we get out of the house, one of the guys will start, 'Lou, honey, don't forget your sweater.'

"I tell him to shut up, and I try to change the subject. I don't understand why she wants to embarrass me like that. I'd never do that to a kid of mine."

The rapid growth spurt of early teen years is as confusing to the parents as it is to the teens. This is a time for two-way tolerance.

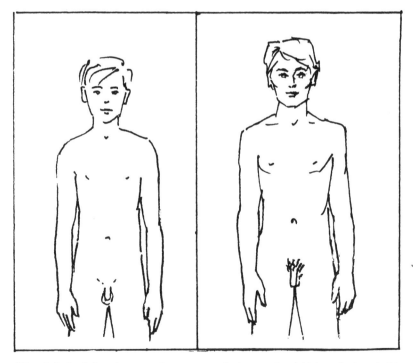

Although both of these boys are the same age, the boy on the right is well along in his development. For the boy on the left, the changes of puberty are starting a little later. He may have a sudden growth spurt and catch up to his friend.

18

Boys' skin problems: Most boys are embarrassed about their skin, too. More than four out of five high school seniors suffer with acne, and many feel ugly, alone, and ashamed. Ralph, who is sixteen, says:

"I like the way my body looks—but my face is a disaster. Pimples all over my map. I wish I could wear a mask to school."

The skin's oil glands are responding to the hormones circulating in the bloodstream and producing the pimples that plague boys, especially, in the teen years. Most young people can cope with their milder conditions, but severe cases may require medical treatment.

"I have hair beginning to grow above my penis and under my arms, but I don't shave yet—and I'm the only guy on the team that doesn't have to. What's wrong with me?"
Each body has its own inner timetable that tells the glands when to start up hormone production (which, in turn, influences the secondary sexual characteristics like hair growth, genital size, and broadening shoulders).

This process began later for you than for your friends, but the likelihood is that you will catch up with them.

"I've heard the guys talk about wet dreams. What are they?"
A wet dream—or, as the books call it, a nocturnal emission—is a natural harmless ejaculation of semen that occurs at night, usually during sleep, often as part of a dream. Semen is a whitish sticky liquid that spurts from the penis at a peak of sexual excitement. The word *ejaculation* means spurting of semen.

"I just ejaculated for the first time. Does that mean that a girl could get pregnant from me?"
Once a boy ejaculates, he is called "sexually developed" because he can now make a girl pregnant.

A female can become pregnant if she has begun to menstruate and if she has sexual intercourse with a boy who has begun to ejaculate.

She can become pregnant even if the penis is withdrawn before ejaculation because some sperm may be in the secretion that seeps out before ejaculation. This is one reason why withdrawal is a poor and dangerous method of contraception.

"Why am I hot all the time, even when I've just jacked off? Why do I get a hard-on when I'm not even thinking about anything sexy? Is that normal?"
Yes, it is normal because most young men have this experience. Some boys get an erection when they work out or do other strenuous exercise.

This is the age when the body is producing a great flood of sex hormones. Because of these hormones many boys cannot help feeling aroused and excited much of the time.

"Some of the guys were fooling around and we started to jack each other off. I liked it, and I think I got a crush on one of the fellows. I want to be near him all the time now. Does that mean I'm a homosexual?"
No, it does not. At your age it is often much easier to start sex play with other boys than it is to approach a girl. While your sexual interest in boys may continue, it is likely that at some point you may find girls more sexually exciting—because that is what most boys experience. But not

CUTAWAY DRAWINGS OF MALE REPRODUCTIVE SYSTEM, ROUTE OF SPERM AND SEMEN

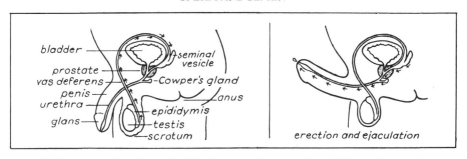

1. Sperm are continuously produced in the testes and mature in the epididymes. Sperm swim up the vas deferens to be stored in the enlarged endings (ampullae).
2. At orgasm, sperm and secretions from the seminal vesicles and prostate are expelled by means of muscular contractions.

all people are alike. It is too soon to know how you will develop.

If it should become clear to you as you get older that it feels more natural to you to be attracted to males rather than females, then it is possible that this preference will continue for the rest of your life. If it does, you may prefer to think of yourself as homosexual (or gay) rather than heterosexual.

It has been estimated that about one out of ten people all over the world are sexually attracted to members of their own sex at some time in their lives. This is true of girls as well as of boys, and of women as well as of men.

"It seems to have happened overnight. Only last term it was easy for me to answer questions in class, and the girls didn't bother me at all. Now, when a teacher calls on me, I feel myself getting red in the face, and I don't know what to say. I'm afraid that if I have to stand up, I could get a hard-on. What am I supposed to do?"
In a state of anxiety about a possible erection you become unable to think straight and unable to know what to say. At your age, erections can appear as a result of excitement, fear, a sexy thought, a girl's smile, or for no reason that you can figure out.

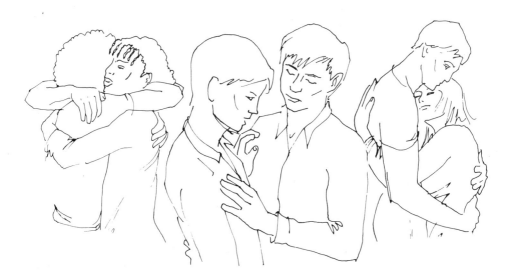

21

Many people blush when they get sexually excited. It's a natural body response.

You've reached biological manhood, along with many of the other boys in the class, and the things you describe are all part of this process.

There is really nothing that you can do to avoid getting an erection, and so you may as well begin to see this experience as an important part of your becoming a man.

"When the other guys talk about their scoring, I don't say anything. I don't know what they're doing or what I'm supposed to do if I like a girl. How do I start?"
The next chapter will talk about the ways that young people become more familiar with their new sexual feelings and learn to enjoy them in ways that do not conflict with their moral values or their plans for the future.

3

Expressing Sexual Feelings

There is no one right way to be sexual. There are many ways to enjoy one's sexual feelings, and this is true for everyone—from the basketball star to the teen in the wheelchair.

Some people have a fine time alone with their imaginations. Other people want to share affection as part of their sexual expression. Still others may want nothing but close physical contact. And for some, the only "right" way to be sexual is to engage in sexual intercourse.

Young people tend to try out whatever feels good to them, whatever they think they are ready for, and whatever their partners find acceptable.

This chapter discusses some of the "Safe Sex" ways in which people of all ages all over the world have been enjoying their sexuality—without sexual intercourse.

"Why do I suddenly want to touch girls?"
Just touching someone you are attracted to can be exciting and satisfying, especially in the early teen years.

It is possible that you may never have thought of touching as an important part of your sexuality. If you grew up in a family where

23

touching was natural, you may find it easy to carry that over into other relationships. Hand holding will be natural to you, and you will reach out easily to hold the hand of someone you like or are attracted to.

Not everybody is so fortunate, though, and some young people may find it difficult to reach out and touch even if it is someone they like very much. At first it may feel awkward, but practice will help. The person whose hand you reach for may be finding it as hard as you to take the first step. But once that step is taken, the result can bring you many joyful moments. For Michael, touch was a new idea:

"I never thought much about touching until I met Grace. My family doesn't go in for touching, I guess. But from the first time I met her, she was always touching my arm or my hand or my shoulder, and I kind of liked it.

"So I started to touch her, too—it felt funny at first, but she seemed to love it. After a while, I got to like it as much as she

did. Now we touch all the time. Funny, it's easier for me to touch other people too.

For centuries people have enjoyed the touching that is part of dancing. When we dance, the inhibitions that keep us from touching are set aside. The more we get used to touching and being touched, the more natural touching becomes. In recent years, the close dancing pattern evolved so that people could enjoy hugging in a socially approved way.

"I've got two left feet. How can I learn to dance?"

One way is to get up and imitate the dancers on TV. Then when you go to a dance, you can imitate the movements of the other kids. Todd remembers his difficulties getting started:

"I used to pretend that I didn't care about dancing, but when the kids got up to dance and I sat there like a jerk, I felt out of it.

"One night when nobody was home, I put a video cassette on and just moved around, trying to do what the guys on the TV did.

Then I tried it in front of a mirror, and I was surprised that it didn't look bad. In fact, it looked pretty good. *I* looked pretty good. Next Friday there's a dance at school. I'm going!"

As you keep dancing, you will probably find that you are developing your own style. You will be enjoying the thrill of your own rhythmic body movement.

"My girlfriend loves close dancing. She could go on all evening. I like it too, but I get so hot that I'm afraid I might come."

Many people like close dancing as their way of being sexual. The slow lovesong can put you in a romantic mood that enhances your feelings for your partner and hers for you. Close dancing is a safe way to enjoy the pleasure of body contact. Males sometimes *do* ejaculate while dancing; it is a common experience.

"I saw a girl at the beach massaging a guy's back. It looked neat to me. How can I learn to give a massage?"

Massage is a good way to break the ice with someone you would like to know better. Or it can be a way of doing something nice for a person you are fond of. Massage is practiced all over the world, often as a sensual experience.

Martin says:

"The only place I could think of to learn more about massage was to go to the library. In the card catalog, I saw lots of books on the subject. Boy, was I surprised. I got one out, and it actually shows you what to do.

"I tried it on my sister when her neck ached. She said it helped, and now everybody in my family asks me to massage their backs and shoulders. I don't mind because it gives me practice. The next time I'm on the beach with a girl I like, I'm going to try it."

Use the library. You can find books on massage by looking up *Massage* in the card catalog. (Most "how-to" books on this subject are

26

numbered 615.822.) They will give you specific directions. If any of your friends has massage experience, you can ask him or her to show you how.

Start by practicing on yourself. That practice can turn into an enjoyable sensual experience with your own body. When you learn what feels good to you, it is easier to guess what other people may enjoy.

"I keep imagining what it would be like to hug and kiss this girl in my class. How can I go about it smoothly?"

Hardly anyone can be smooth in a situation like this, and it is unfair to demand it of yourself. Accept your feeling of awkwardness and realize that the girl may feel awkward, too. Besides, some girls even dislike a smooth approach.

It may be a good idea to tell her that you would like to hug and kiss her. She may be pleased. Hugging and kissing can be an expression of friendship or affection. But it can also be an unthreatening way of enjoying sexual feelings.

Awkwardness is the human condition. Many boys are timid about approaching girls and showing interest. Many girls are timid, too, but they are less bothered by this feeling because girls have generally been taught that it is better for them to act shyly than to act assertively. This often puts females at a disadvantage.

Fear of rejection is enough to discourage many young people from expressing affection or sexual interest. But rejection at one time or another is unavoidable—and we do recover.

"I think the idea of 'french' kissing is disgusting. Do I have to do it if I have a date?"

No, of course not. Although some young people like "french" kissing (sometimes called tongue kissing, soul kissing, or deep kissing), some others don't like it at all. These days tongue kissing may be risky because the contagious STDs (sexually transmitted diseases) are now so common.

The problem of lip sores: It is wise to be aware of any sore on your lip or on the lip of the person you want to kiss. Contact with a lip sore is an easy way of transmitting or acquiring a contagious disease like herpes.

If there is such a sore, you can hug all you like—but put off the kissing until it is gone. Some lip sores are signs of STDs and need medical attention. (See Chapter Eight, page 95.)

"My friends talk about 'light petting' and 'heavy petting.' What's the difference?"
Usually "light petting" means affectionate stroking of the body above the waist—like "necking." "Heavy petting" is another term for "making out, but not going all the way" or "fooling around." It usually starts as light petting and then, as one or both partners get more excited,

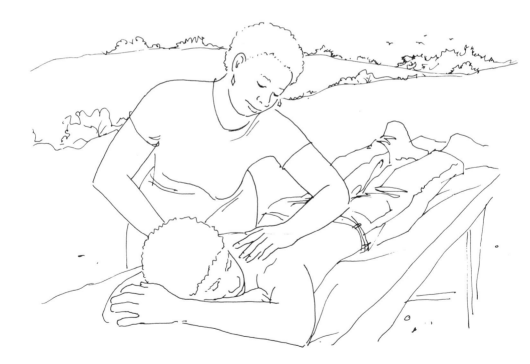

the stroking extends to the sex organs, and to masturbation of one or both partners (sometimes called "mutual masturbation"). It may or may not result in orgasm for one or both partners.

Many religious educators and sex educators are now urging young people to refrain from heavy petting. They believe that it inevitably leads to high-risk behavior like sexual intercourse—that people lose control when aroused sexually, and forget their carefully made decisions. This does happen most frequently when partners are using alcohol or drugs.

Sheila, a sophomore in high school, talks about petting and her thoughts about "going all the way":

"One of the things I like best about Tom is that he's not pushing me. I know he gets excited; so do I, but we love to neck and pet until we both come. I think Tom would like it if I said, 'Let's do it tonight,' but somehow, I don't feel ready and I don't want to have to worry about whether I get my period.

"I think I want to wait till I get married but I'm only fifteen and I don't know if Tom is the guy I'll want to marry.

"My sister—she's eighteen—says I'll change my mind when I get to college. I'm not sure."

"I don't know if I have an orgasm or not. What is it supposed to feel like?"

Orgasm (or "coming") means the pleasurable climax that results from a buildup of sexual excitement, muscle tension and spasms, and then release of tension. In males it is usually accompanied by ejaculation (shooting semen).

Most boys have practiced stimulating themselves to orgasm through masturbation. Many girls, too, have brought themselves to orgasm (or "climax") through masturbation.

Other girls "come" for the first time when they are sexually stimulated by a partner. They may then try it themselves. These girls are developing their own patterns of sexual response as a social reaction to a partner. Elise, who is fifteen, says:

"I met this guy Gary when I was spending the summer with my grandmother in Chicago, and I really liked him. We saw a lot of each other, and gradually we began to make out. I had my first orgasm with him, and from then on, I couldn't get enough petting and necking. When the end of August came and I had to go home, I hated to leave him.

"A couple of nights after I got home, I decided to do to myself what Gary did to me. I didn't come as fast, but when I did come, it felt just as wonderful. I felt so lucky that I had discovered how to touch myself down there. For a while I thought I was the only girl in the world with a special secret.

"Then school began and I had this sexuality course. That's when I learned that I had been masturbating. 'So that's what masturbation is,' I thought. I wasn't the only girl in the world who knew how to do it, after all."

The boys, however, have typically spent several years alone practicing and developing *their* response patterns without a partner.

"Why do boys and girls seem to have such different ideas about sex and love?"

The different ways in which many boys and girls initially develop their patterns of sexual response—solitary for boys, in a partner situation for girls—lead to important differences between men and women.

Another reason is that, beginning in childhood, males and females are taught traditional conflicting sex roles that define how they should think and behave about love and sex.

Then, as a result of these differences in early development, when boys and girls, men and women, come together in a sexual situation, they may feel that they speak different languages and that they are trying to communicate with members of another species.

"Why does the talking always stop when you start making out?"

The difficulties in attempting communication make it tempting to fall into sexual play as if driven by some mechanical force, that people think of as "passion."

Recognizing that differences do exist between male and female may make it easier to persist in trying to communicate. Practice may not make perfect, but practice will help.

"I keep seeing the word 'masturbation,' but what exactly does it mean?"

Masturbation means stroking the genital organs for pleasure. Males stroke the penis; females usually stimulate the labia and clitoris. It leads to feelings of arousal and excitement and usually results in orgasm. For some, masturbation is followed by a sense of quiet satisfaction. For some others, it is often followed by a feeling of uneasiness or guilt.

SELF-EXAMINATION WITH A MIRROR

It is important to get to know how your genitals look. The lips can be spread to see the vagina, the urethra, and the clitoris.

How you feel about masturbation depends on how you were brought up, how your parents reacted to your childhood genital touching, on their religious beliefs, and on the attitudes of your friends.

You hear varied opinions about masturbation. Some religions teach that masturbation is sinful, and some members of these denominations do not masturbate and believe that it is wrong for others to enjoy their sexuality in this way. Most people outside of these religious denominations do not consider masturbation "wrong." Some, however, think that it is an inferior way of expressing one's sexuality—inferior to partner sex. This judgment is based on tradition. In this Age of AIDS, STDs, and widespread unplanned pregnancy, it is important to reexamine these judgments—in order to stay alive, healthy, and unburdened by childcare, at least until past one's teen years.

There seem to be dozens of slang terms for the word *masturbate*. Some of them are "jack off," "jerk off," and "play with yourself." We sometimes hear them used as put-down expressions, when young people tease each other.

There are people who are not embarrassed about their pleasure in their own bodies. Others are secret about their personal sexual experience; most people want privacy. Alan, who is now sixteen, says:

"I've been jerking off for years—since I was about eight—but I always did it in private, in the bathroom or locked in my own room. Then one day, I was on my bed with my eyes closed, pumping away, when I heard the door open and my brother stood there—he's twenty. I grabbed the covers and pulled them over me.

" 'Damn it! Can't you knock?' I yelled.

"But all he said was, 'Sorry. Next time I will. Hey, Alan—don't be embarrassed. Everybody does it.' "

"He grinned, and as he went out the door he said, 'Don't forget to knock when you come in my room.' "

Of course, not *everybody* does do it. Besides those who refrain because of religious beliefs, some people just happen to have scant production of sex hormones, and they have little or no interest in being sexual.

Most people begin in infancy to fondle their genitals. Some continue to find comfort and pleasure in masturbation all their lives. It is a way of being sexual that can start in early years and go on through old age.

People use a variety of methods, but most adopt some few techniques that work for them and hardly vary them for the rest of their lives.

"How do girls masturbate?"

Many girls stroke around the clitoris and genital lips (or labia). They may start by stroking the inner thighs, the outer genital lips (or labia majora), the pubic mound, and the breasts. They may then wet the area around the clitoris with saliva or with some of the moisture from the vagina. The wetness gives a more sensual feeling and prevents irritation.

While some girls like to stroke the exposed glans of the clitoris, others find the clitoris too sensitive for direct touch. Delicate touch may feel good at one moment, firm touch at another.

"If you just squeeze your thighs but don't touch yourself down there, is that still called masturbation?"

When the purpose is to feel erotic arousal, this is a type of masturbation. Some girls squeeze thighs together rhythmically and sometimes reach orgasm this way.

Contrary to the belief commonly held by boys, very few females insert objects (like dildos or cucumbers) into their vaginas for sexual stimulation.

"If a girl gets used to a vibrator, does she get so she needs it to have an orgasm? Could she get addicted?"

No, people do not get addicted to vibrators. Most find them arousing for a while and then seem to forget about them. When partners use them, care should be taken to avoid exchange of vaginal secretions or semen from one person to another. Another caution: never use a vibrator in the bathtub or shower.

The small battery-operated penis-shaped vibrators are most popular. They are not usually used as penis substitutes—for insertion and thrusting. Women use them to stimulate nipples, clitoris and labia, and the whole skin. Men use them the same way, on the entire body surface.

"Can a vibrator be used in the anus?"
Unless it is a specially made anal stimulator with a lip or flange to keep it from slipping into the rectum, a vibrator should not be inserted in the anus. People sometimes do lose an object in the rectum and then a doctor is needed to remove it.

"Is it true some girls have an orgasm just by playing with their breasts?"
Yes, it is, and some men, too, become highly aroused, but most men never develop this breast responsiveness. Some wheelers, women and men with spine injuries who have lost sensation below the chest and in their sex organs, are able to develop sexual sensitivity in other parts of their body—for example, in the breasts, neck, shoulders, or ears— so that they can again experience an intense sexual climax.

"My girlfriends talk about 'rubbing off,' but I think it is immoral and disgusting. Am I so unusual?"
There are wide differences in interest and in attitudes toward masturbation. A large minority of females never masturbate. Among women who do, there is great variation in the techniques used and in how much time is devoted to it. Women may spend minutes or hours; they may masturbate often, infrequently, or never at all.

"Do all boys masturbate the same way?"
Most boys grasp the penis with one hand and stroke it up and down— some slowly, others rapidly, some lightly, others firmly. Usually, as

arousal increases, movements become more rapid. Some boys add rhythmic pelvic thrusting movements and muscle tensing.

There is no typical posture. They may be sitting, standing, kneeling, squatting, or lying. Some boys masturbate by lying on their bellies making thrusting movements against a bedsheet or pillow. Masturbation is usually accompanied by fantasy—with pictures, fiction, or memories.

Boys often ask: "How often is it 'normal' to masturbate? What happens if you masturbate 'too much'?"
There is no such thing as too much or too little. If the male or female genitals should get sore from frequent handling, they will heal in a day or so. However, some people never masturbate, feel no need or interest, and seem to experience no ill effects from their abstinence.

"Why doesn't everybody do it?"
Some religious teachers believe that masturbation is sinful. Other religious counselors state that the capacity for sexual pleasure is a gift from God, and that the freedom to enjoy one's own body is a precious right. Young people who feel in conflict about this subject may do well to discuss it with their parents and with their religious counselors.

"I can control myself most of the time, and I don't abuse myself because of my moral beliefs. Sometimes, though, when I'm alone in the house, I get really stoned. Then I lose control and jack off, and I'm terribly ashamed afterwards. How can I get better self-control?"
Most people lose self-control when they are stoned. A first step to self-control is to learn how to enjoy living sober and drug-free. If this isn't possible for you, discuss your conflict with a parent, a youth counselor, or your religious advisor.

"My boyfriend read in a magazine that a safe way to be sexual is to masturbate together, side by side. I feel funny about it—isn't masturbation supposed to be private?"

Ours is a society in which many viewpoints can be expressed—from the most conservative to the most liberal. Magazines and television express a variety of viewpoints, and speak to many different kinds of listeners and readers. The magazine article was certainly addressed to adults, and was concerned with helping people to stay healthy.

Since many boys masturbate together in their early teens, the idea of side by side masturbation with a girlfriend may have seemed natural enough, but if it conflicts with your beliefs about what is "right," then you must follow your own conscience.

Eric, who is a senior in a Berkeley high school, saw a video film of a gay "Safe Sex Party":

"It started off like any party except there was no beer or dope and there were no girls—there were only guys. Then they started fooling around with each other, like in a locker room sometimes, but they really got into it, and you could tell they were excited over each other.

"I never saw anything like that—they started jerking each other off and kissing and hugging a lot. They were playing around with condoms though they were only jacking off. It really blew my mind."

These boys seem to have given up their need for privacy and have found an unconventional way of enjoying a social yet safe type of sexual expression.

Another safe experience that some young people enjoy is taking a shower or bathing together. Showering together affords a good opportunity to check out bodies for signs of infection.

Of course if either of you has any signs that indicate a possible sexually transmitted infection (see Chapter Eight), it is best to put off any genital contacts until a doctor has been consulted.

But you can still talk about what you need to do now. You can plan your trip to a clinic or to a private physician, and you may want to go together. Talking about the problem and doing something about it will probably bring you closer to each other.

"I get a kick out of talking about sex. Is that kinky?"
There is nothing kinky about sex talk. It is fun and safe, and it comes in many varieties. There is romantic sex talk—like in the old movies. There is hot sex talk—about what you would like to do to each other. And there is sexy shared fantasy: couples can make up their private scenarios just for the fun of their turn-on.

"How can I find out what the other kids are really doing and what certain words mean?"
Perhaps the most important kind of sex talk is the sharing of sex information. Friends share, parents sometimes share, youth counselors

For many people, being alone with themselves in the bath or the shower is a favorite way to enjoy sensual feeling.

share, and the telephone information hotlines provide answers to sex questions. The "other kids" are not usually candid about their own experience and their state of ignorance. But there are surveys of teen sex behavior, and you'll find them in the public library.

When you need accurate and reliable sex information quickly, there are community sex hotlines in the large cities and also national phone information hotlines (with toll-free 800 numbers) that will answer your questions about the health aspects of sex. They are staffed by friendly, well-trained volunteers. Some of these hotlines are listed on pages 114 and 115. Well-informed teens now have their own hotline: 1-800-234-TEEN, 5 P.M. to 9 P.M. EDT.

TALKING OF LOVE IN AMERICAN SIGN LANGUAGE

Talk of sensuality, of sexuality, and of love is one of the joys of the hearing impaired, and the signing vocabulary of sexuality is extensive and expressive.

38

"When I want to turn on, I take out my picture of this rock singer and I make believe I'm a drummer in the band and then we get it on together. This is my favorite scene, and I get hot just thinking about it. Is it crazy to have thoughts like this?"

There is nothing crazy about enjoying fantasy. Most people have them every day. Fantasy is a way that many people use to enjoy themselves sexually. People's fantasies range from the simplest memory to the most outlandish kind of scenario. Paul describes his turn-on:

"When I jack off, I'm in another world. Sometimes I'm an emperor like Genghis Khan, and I'm a tough ruler—I hurt people and get all excited when they are scared of me. Me—I have trouble stepping on an ant! But then sometimes I'm the Emperor and the Slave at the same time and I get excited when I imagine I'm being tied up."

Almost anything can trigger the imagination: space comics, pictures in rock-'n'-roll magazines, scenes in romantic novels, music on the radio, MTV, and memories of episodes in movies and of real-life personal experiences. Andrea says:

"When I fantasize, I become an entirely different person. I believe in women's rights and all that, and I don't let anyone step on me in real life. But one day I picked up one of the romances my sister likes—there was this macho guy who raped the girl who became his slave. I got so hot, I came while reading.

"Now, when I masturbate, that's my fantasy—I'm the girl enslaved by that brute. It embarrasses me just to think about it, but once the fantasy starts, I'm lost. I tell myself—'It's just a fantasy.' If any guy tried to hurt me in real life, I'd fracture him!"

"Sometimes when I kiss my boyfriend, I close my eyes and imagine I'm kissing Bruce Springsteen. Then I feel guilty and wonder if there's something wrong with me."

Almost everyone has this type of fantasy. Some people use the same fantasy lover over and over again while others try out a dozen different ones. This is a safe way of enjoying a variety of partners without the risk of getting infected by a variety of sexually transmitted diseases.

"Am I being unfaithful to my partner?" is a troubling question. But fantasy is harmless. Since there is no way to push these fantasy thoughts out of mind—even if we wanted to—it makes sense to enjoy the turn-on without feeling guilty.

Meanwhile, your boyfriend may be happily imagining that he is kissing Madonna.

"My cousin told me about a nude beach he went to. He said it was great, and he asked me to go with him. I'll feel self-conscious because I'm not really well hung."
Most boys seem to have that same concern. And almost every boy thinks that his penis is smaller than it really is because of the angle from which he looks at it. To others it looks larger—not that it should matter.

Learn to like your own body and all its parts. Your genitals may not yet be fully grown, but even if they are, it's important for you to learn to accept and come to like every single part of your body, including your sex organs and your anus.

Nude beaches are not only for "the beautiful people." They are for everyone who chooses the experience, including the girl who thinks that her breasts are too small and her thighs too heavy, as well as the boy who does not consider himself "well hung." On a nude beach people see all kinds of bodies and become tolerant of all the imperfections of other bodies and even of their own imperfect bodies.

"My boyfriend and I used to spend a lot of time kissing and necking and hugging, and I loved all of it. Then one night we went all the way. Now that's all we do. We never neck anymore, and I miss it. If I brought it up, I know what he'd say, 'That's kid stuff.' Am I being immature?"
There is nothing immature about longing for a kind of experience that

used to give you pleasure. What you describe seems to be a common pattern among partners of all ages.

Once people start having intercourse, they seem to start bypassing all the caressing that they used to enjoy. But they are short-changing themselves when they think of the sexual intercourse orgasm as their goal. This is the time to start talking. If you are close enough to have intercourse, certainly you are close enough to talk about anything that is important to you.

It is mature to ask for what you want and to say clearly what you believe. It is your right to pursue your desires and to express them freely, especially to someone you feel so close to.

"I saw a newspaper story that talked about Safe Sex, but everything the article mentioned was either kid stuff or kind of kinky. I just want to have real sex. I'm not gay, so what does 'Safe Sex' have to do with guys like me?"
Nowadays we frequently see the expression "Safe Sex" (or "Safer Sex," which has the same meaning) on posters and in magazines

and books. "Safe Sex" means any kind of sexual interaction in which we protect ourselves and our partners from the risk of AIDS and other STDs. "Safe Sex" includes a broad range of sexual activities—from kissing and hugging to intercourse with a condom for the male and one of the contraceptive foams or the Today Sponge for the female.

The belief that AIDS strikes only gay men may give some people comfort, but it is a false notion. About 23 percent of the men who have died from AIDS were heterosexual.

Another fact is that more than a quarter of the people with AIDS are intravenous drug users (people who shoot drugs with shared needles), most of whom are not gay. The most rapid increases in AIDS cases are occurring among IV drug users and in the teenage segment of the population.

In addition, heterosexual men and women have been contracting AIDS through sexual intercourse with partners who had shot up drugs in the past, long before the sexual contact.

This is why "Safe Sex" must be a concern for everybody, including young men who just want "real sex," meaning sexual intercourse. Even they can learn to modify their behavior to suit the times.

The idea of "Safe Sex" is not new. In the seventies it referred to ways of expressing sexuality other than having intercourse. Today, for those who reject the option of abstinence, "Safe Sex" becomes the way to reduce health risks and at the same time to make sexual experience more varied and exciting.

"My big thrill is when I score. I've out-grown kissing and holding hands and playing with myself. How could I go back to kid stuff now?"

The goal of "scoring" is an out-dated one. It is left over from the days when young men thought of sex as conquest rather than as a way of having pleasure and giving pleasure. It is the idea of "scoring" that has become "kid stuff."

Pete's priorities are different from those of his circle of friends. Pete says:

> "I'm getting sick of the guys and the way they brag about scoring. It's just not something I want to do right now. I've got college and med school ahead of me, and I don't want to get involved.
>
> "They tease me about still being a virgin—and a couple of times I said, 'You're crazy. I just don't like to brag.' But my best friend, Ed, knows the truth."

A boy does not become a "man" the moment he puts his penis in somebody's vagina. To "be a man" means to have the ability to act responsibly towards himself—and towards others. The boy becomes a "man" when he no longer thinks only of immediate gratification, but plans for his future—for satisfying personal relations and for interesting work.

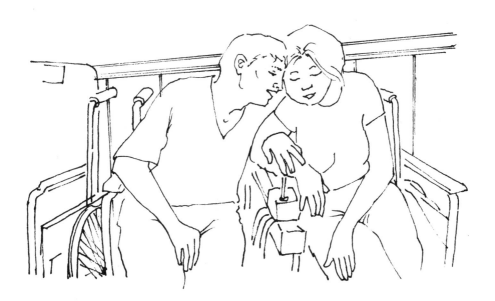

"My girlfriends tease me about still being a virgin. Sometimes I think I'll go find just any guy so I won't be a virgin anymore." Some girls today feel embarrassed about being virgins and look for an opportunity to lose their virginity "spontaneously" because they believe that having sexual intercourse makes them "real women."

It does not. What makes a girl into a "woman" is the realization that her body is her own and that she has the right to choose how she wants to use it and how she wants (or doesn't want) to be sexual. She does not want to be burdened with an infant before she has completed her education and prepared for a satisfying life, whether as a mature homemaker or in a career or occupation outside the home.

Human beings have always sought comfort and pleasure in moments of physical closeness. These moments help us to endure

the frustrations, the bad luck, the painful experiences that happen to all of us. Human contacts, whether just an eager glance, a brushing of lips, or an embrace, are joys that enrich our lives.

* * *

The next chapter discusses another aspect of growing up—figuring out how far you want to go and how much you are willing to risk. This chapter will help you work out your sexual decisions and your plans for seeing them through.

4

Thinking About Sexual Decisions

"Too many things are happening too fast! I don't even know what I want. How can I know what's right for me?"

You have reached a stage of life that you have been looking forward to for some time. Now that you are there, it may seem overwhelming, but this chapter will try to help you sort things out. It will put the many choices into sharper focus, but the decisions will be yours.

Plotting your own sex life is like plotting a play—and you are the writer, the director, as well as the actor.

One teen says, "I couldn't wait to start dating. The other kids say I'm boy-crazy and my parents worry about me. Isn't it normal to like boys?" Another teen says, "All my friends have started dating, but I just don't want to go out with boys yet. What if someone asks me?" Everyone is different, and you have the right to think for yourself and make up your own mind about whom you want to date and whether you want to date at all. It is normal to like boys, and it is equally normal to want nothing to do with them.

It is up to you to write your own script. If a boy asks you to go out with him and it is not something you want to do, you can simply tell him so. He has a right to ask, but you have an equal right to refuse. You may get interested next month, next year, or you may never choose to date.

At your age young people feel uncomfortable about being different. But the fact is that every person is unique, and recognizing that you are not exactly like everyone else is an important step in growing up.

"My boyfriend keeps pressuring me to start having sex now. Is there anything wrong with not going all the way until you're married?"

Of course not! There is nothing wrong about putting off sexual intercourse until marriage—for whatever reason you may have. It may even be the best decision you could possibly make at this point in your life. It is the only sure way to avoid AIDS and other STDs and unplanned pregnancy. Some young people decide on the basis of religious beliefs—going against one's religious beliefs causes guilt and confusion. Others may decide to abstain from intercourse in order to avoid conflict with parents or conflict with the values of their community.

Although your decision is right for you, your boyfriend's behavior in exerting psychological pressure is clearly wrong.

You can make it clear to your boyfriend that you want to wait, and you can ask him to stop pressuring you. If he persists, you will be learning things about him that you need to know, and you may decide that this is not someone you want to be intimate with in any way.

You can practice saying "yes" to what you want and "no" to what you don't want. And you can begin to practice asking for what you would like. If, for example, what you want is to keep a relationship at a hand-holding stage, it is right for you to say so.

For many girls, and for boys as well, asserting one's opinions, intentions, and desires has to be learned through conscious practice. If it seems difficult because assertiveness is not part of your early training, start with small assertions—and keep practicing.

Everyone benefits. The chances are that your boyfriend will welcome the increased communication between you.

Barbara tells about her experience with saying, "No!"

"I was out with Stuart—a first date, and we were in his car after the movie when he grabbed me and started to move his hands all over my body. 'Stuart, stop,' I said. But he didn't. He just kept doing it, and I realized that he wasn't listening to what I was saying at all.

"Finally, I just pulled away from him and pushed him hard. I yelled 'No!' Well, he stopped and looked kind of ashamed. Then he said, 'I guess I thought I was supposed to . . . I thought a girl always said 'No' even when she didn't mean it.'

"I never expected what happened. We began to talk, really talk, and he turned out to be a nice guy. Now, he's one of my best friends."

"I am definitely waiting for marriage to have sex. Is there any reason why I should have to take the sexuality course in my high school?"

Regardless of your plans for the future, it is your responsibility to learn as much as you can about safe sexual behaviors, about contraception and STD prevention—because many unplanned pregnancies happen unexpectedly to girls who, like you, had been determined to put off intercourse until marriage. The more that you learn now, the less likely it is that you will find yourself in a situation that you cannot control.

Passion may be overwhelming. It is easy, especially if you are petting, to get caught up in the excitement of the moment and to give in to your partner's persuasion.

Although they may have had no intention of having intercourse, many young people (both girls and boys) have their first intercourse experience imposed on them by another person—often an older teen, and sometimes an adult. An older person may have great skill at persuasion. This is one of the significant reasons for young people to learn how to speak up and say what they want, or do not want, forcefully enough to convince anybody—friends, dates, or older people—that they mean what they say.

Failing to speak honestly to one another leads to confusion between boys and girls just as it does between men and women.

"If you want to have sex with a girl, do you have to pretend that you love her?"
In the long run it works out better when you do not pretend that your feelings are any different than they are. A young man who pretends love is being foolishly dishonest because he may find himself trapped in a relationship that he will then have to struggle to get out of.

"I heard a sex therapist on the radio. She said sex is only satisfying when you're in love with your partner. I don't love anybody, but I do like sex. Was she exaggerating?"
Yes. Her statement is not strictly true. Some people do enjoy sex

without love. Many who have grown up with the belief that sex is immoral find it difficult to enjoy being sexual with the people they love. But most mature people find great satisfaction in the combination of love and sex in marriage.

"The guys say that when a girl says 'no' she really means 'yes.' Why?"
This is a false impression that causes a great deal of trouble between men and women. When girls say "no," they usually mean it, just as boys do. When boys act on their misinformation, forcing sex on girls who resist, they are committing a crime of violence—date rape or acquaintance rape.

"If you're gay do you have to date girls and pretend you're going all the way with them so people won't know?"
No, not if you get no pleasure from the company of girls. It is probably better not to waste your time with dating and devote it to whatever you find truly absorbing. Of course if you value a girl's friendship, enjoy it, and forget about what people may think.

"Do you have to pretend you're not interested in sex so that when you start having sex, it will seem spontaneous?"
No. Romantic spontaneity was a value in the Pre-AIDS Age. Today it is absurd. It was always something of a myth, anyway, because the "spontaneous" sexual act usually followed long planning on the part of the young man, and sometimes on the part of the young woman, too.

Questions involving pretense come up because young people get conflicting and confusing messages about sex. Each of these last few questions involves deception and pretense. But we are threatened by AIDS and other STDs and it is necessary to give up lies and risky game-playing—and to substitute candor and straight talk.

Sexual dishonesty is too dangerous a game for anyone to play in the Age of AIDS!

"Whenever I bring up sex at home my mother acts embarrassed, so I've stopped trying to talk to her about the subject. I can talk about sex with my girlfriends, but I'd be embarrassed to death to talk to a guy about sex."

During the teen years embarrassment seems to be one's daily companion. Somehow your mother's generation "got by" with little talk about sex. But your generation faces threats that were unknown just a few years ago. The threat of AIDS makes it absolutely necessary to fight the embarrassment that most people feel when approaching an unfamiliar subject. Persistence and practice will help you conquer your feelings of awkwardness.

Your generation may be the first in your family to start talking candidly about sex. Your parents may still believe the myth that they were taught—that it is positively dangerous for young people to have any sexual knowledge. But you can help your parents and help yourself. Introduce the subject over and over again until it loses its power to threaten.

Reading as much as you can about sex, especially in young-adult books in the library, will make you more comfortable with the subject. Then you can bring it up in discussions with your friends. This is the way Phyllis broke the ice with her friends:

"I had been doing a lot of reading, and I was dying to talk to my friends about the different ideas I was getting, but I was afraid they'd put me down. In a sex information book, I read that the best way to begin is simply to start talking and to try to get other kids talking, too.

"One night I was at a party and somebody brought up AIDS. That was my cue. I started in with what I had been reading, and just like the book said, other kids started to talk, too. Pretty soon, almost everybody was joining in, and later a lot of us felt that it was the best party we had been to in a long time. Some of the kids really revealed fears they had never mentioned to anyone before."

The chances are that your friends feel as uncomfortable about starting to talk as you do, but the only way to decrease that discomfort is to keep talking and exchanging information.

Learn all you can about all the ways that people are sexual—whether you are presexual, heterosexual, bisexual, homosexual, or nonsexual—so that you can be tolerant of your own emerging sexual desires and those of other people whose desires may be very different from yours.

The more you learn from books, the more you will realize how widespread sexual ignorance is. An example of misinformation is the way the words "normal" and "abnormal" are bandied about. It seems that most young people worry about whether or not they have normal sexual responses, normal sexual fantasies, normal sexual organs, normal sexual relations, are normal in their sexual preferences, or normal in their lack of sexual interest.

At the same time they tend to judge everyone else's normalcy in spite of the confusion about what is "normal."

"How do you know what is normal?"
The words "normal" and "abnormal" are simply not useful standards in judging either your own or anyone else's sexuality. In human sexuality there is such a wide range of patterns—habits of behavior, desires, fantasies, sexual preference—that no two people are exactly alike.

"Normal" and "abnormal" have no clear meaning in relation to sex. When people say that something is abnormal, they usually mean that they dislike it or disapprove of it.

"In the past year my best friend has really gotten into classical music and all he does is play the flute. The guys call him queer and they've begun to say I must be queer too because I stick up for him."
The word "queer," like the word "abnormal," is frequently meant as a put-down. Sometimes it is used to imply that someone is "peculiar," not like everybody else.

The young person who gets absorbed in some personal hobby or artistic effort is fortunate because this kind of absorbing interest makes for a satisfying sort of life.

Most young people, though, tend to want to appear like "everyone else." Therefore, the individualist who doesn't conform or who becomes absorbed in an interest that the others do not share is likely to be labeled "queer."

But the label "queer" is also used to mean "having a sexual preference for persons of the same sex." Since a significant minority of the male population is sexually interested in other males, this tendency is really not so unusual. Most teens, however, find this interest hard to understand.

Steve, who is in high school now, has been aware since third grade that he gets excited about other boys the way most boys react to girls. He talks matter-of-factly about it:

"I like girls—to talk to—I'm even attracted by one occasionally, but nothing like the way I react to Ron. When he smiles at me a certain way, it really turns me on.

"I talked to my mother about it because she started asking questions like, 'Why don't you ever go to the dances? Isn't the Junior Prom coming up?'

"So I told her, 'I'd go if I could go with Ron.' At first she acted as if she didn't understand, but finally she did. And then she began to tell me I'd grow out of it. 'Wait a while,' she said. 'You may meet a lovely girl.'

"There's no point in saying, 'I have, Mom, dozens of them—but nothing happens for me.'

"Ron and I have decided to go to the same college, but until then we've got to hide what we feel for each other."

As many as one-third of all males have sex contacts with other males at some times in their lives, many before they begin to be sexual with females. They are not necessarily homosexual; most do not consider themselves gay. Some of these males marry and enjoy their married sex lives and their families while they continue to find sexual pleasure in other males from time to time.

Some girls, too, enjoy sex play with other girls—often before they become sexual with boys. If they go on preferring women as their sexual partners, they call themselves lesbian. Jacqueline describes her experience:

"When I was little, I liked to be called Jackie. I liked boys, and I liked to play boys' games. But in high school I decided that Jacqueline was a really pretty name, and my friends stopped calling me Jackie.

"When the other girls were starting to date, I felt out of step. I didn't want to start dating. I was getting crushes—but not on boys.

"It scared me enough so that I began to pretend I was like all the other girls, and I went out with guys all the time. I especially liked double-dating—because of the other girl we were with. The guys I dated were OK, but they didn't turn me on.

"Then one night I decided to go all the way with Joe—someone I liked and had been seeing for a while. I thought maybe actually having sex would do it for me and cure the way I felt about girls. When it was over, I felt like crying. As much as I liked Joe, I didn't want to do what I was doing with him.

"But just the thought of touching Marie thrilled me. I began to read about lesbians, and there I was in the books, and there were lots of other girls like me. That did it for me. I was through pretending. I knew that I was a lesbian and that I would be one all my life."

"I read someone got AIDS from a bisexual. How do you recognize them?"

You can't identify a bisexual by appearance any more than you can expect to recognize someone who is lesbian or gay or straight. You can get AIDS from anyone—heterosexual, homosexual, or bisexual—who is infected with the AIDS virus, but if you take Safe Sex precautions, you minimize your risks no matter who your partner may be.

By Safe Sex precautions we mean any of the sexual behaviors that were described in Chapter Three and also the barrier methods that we will be describing in Chapter Six for people who are having sexual intercourse.

"What does bisexual mean?"

A bisexual is a male or female who chooses to have sexual contact with both males and females (usually at different times). Some people's sex preferences change at different stages of their lives.

Rita, who is now fifteen, thinks that she may be bisexual.

"I've been going out with boys since I was fourteen, and I like being with a boy very much. But then one day I met Dorothy, and I found myself dreaming about her. In my dream, we did what I've read lesbians do, and it was wonderful.

"But when I went out with Craig, I was as excited about him as I've ever been, and I liked kissing and touching him, too. I

guess I want to try both girls and guys. Maybe I'll never be able to choose one over the other.

"I used to wonder what bisexuals looked like. Now I know— like everybody else!"

* * *

When young people think over their decisions about their own sexual interests, the thought of AIDS is always in the background. There is reason for concern about AIDS, but no need for fear. We need to replace anxiety with knowledge; the next chapter summarizes what we know about AIDS today.

5

Facts About AIDS

"Why is this disease called AIDS?"
The name is derived from the initials of Acquired Immune Deficiency Syndrome. (See "Words and Meanings," page 116, for explanations of words that are unfamiliar.)

"Is AIDS really a threat to everybody?"
AIDS is a threat to everyone who shares needles for intravenous drug injections or other purposes and to anyone who is sexually active, with the exception of couples who have had no other sexual contacts for at least eight years. At present, there is no cure for it, nor is any vaccine available. We can hope that the AIDS research going on now will, within the next few years, lead to some breakthrough—either a vaccine that will protect us or a cure.

Until that time, however, the spread of AIDS can be controlled if people become informed about the specific dangers. And so you need to know how it is transmitted from person to person and how it attacks the body.

Information and education are the only weapons against AIDS. Armed with the facts on AIDS, we can stop its spread, avoid or reduce personal risk, and know that we have little to fear.

"Can you catch AIDS if you're too close to someone who has it?"
There is no risk from casual contact. Family members living with people with AIDS do not become infected. Clyde's experience is one that many of us may be sharing in one form or another.

"A few months ago my best friend, Tony, told me that his brother, Hank, was so sick he had to leave school. I knew that Hank had been a heavy drug user, but I hadn't seen him for a while. When I did see him, I was shocked at the way he looked—all thin and pale with blotches on his skin. Finally Tony told me that his brother had AIDS.

"I went crazy, thinking, My God, I shook hands with the guy. I wiped my hands on a towel in the bathroom. Was I next? At first, Tony couldn't understand why I refused to come to his house the way I always had. He's no dope, though, and we've been friends for a long time.

"He mailed me an article about AIDS that he had cut out of a scientific magazine. That was where I learned that you don't get AIDS by shaking somebody's hand or using his towel.

"It got my head straight again, and now I see Hank whenever I go to Tony's. We talk a lot, too, and he seems to like my being there. Now he talks to me as if I were his age instead of his little brother's friend. We don't talk about his disease much, but he keeps warning me not to do drugs. Ever!"

AIDS is a disease that weakens the body's ability to fight off other diseases. Defense against disease is the job of the body's *immune system.*

"What is the 'immune system'?"
The immune system is the body's defense mechanism for warding off disease and infection. The body's "soldiers" are the white blood cells that produce antibodies (tiny protein substances) to fight germs. Normally we are not affected by these germs that are all around us and even live in our bodies.

When the immune system is weakened, *opportunistic infections* can get a foothold and develop. These are infections that ordinarily would not affect a healthy body but can take advantage of a vulnerable immune system to invade and eventually kill a person weakened by the AIDS virus.

"What kind of diseases do people with AIDS get?"
The most common of these opportunistic infections is *pneumocystis carinii* pneumonia—a parasitic infection of the lungs. Other AIDS-related diseases are a neurological disease that causes brain damage, tuberculosis, and Kaposi's sarcoma (a formerly rare cancer of the blood vessels).

Persons who care for AIDS patients at home should try to make the patients as comfortable as possible and protect them from infection. Brad, a seventeen-year-old, was unaware—as many of us are—of how vulnerable a person with AIDS is. He tells of his experience:

"My cousin, Don, has AIDS, and I visit him often. Last week, when I rang the bell, his brother, Nick, opened the door. I had a cold for a few days, and I was coughing.

"Nick said, 'Do you have a cold?' I nodded my head in the middle of a cough. 'You can't see Don until you're okay,' he said. 'I'm not going to get AIDS because I have a cold,' I said, laughing.

"But Nick was very serious. 'I'm not worried about you,' he said. 'If Don got your cold, he could develop pneumonia. His immune system is damaged. He can't take chances getting anything.' Then he added, 'You've just got a cold, but Don could die.'

" 'I'm sorry,' I said, and I was. 'Tell Don I'll see him next week—when I'm over this. Never mind, I'll tell him myself on the phone later.' "

"How do you get AIDS?"
AIDS is caused by a virus, which is a kind of microscopic germ that

reproduces itself only in living cells (as in the human body) and causes disease.

First diagnosed in this country in 1981, AIDS presented a puzzling problem to scientists. Since most of those first diagnosed as having AIDS were gay men, it was mistakenly believed that some factor in a gay lifestyle was causing the disease. But in 1984 medical scientists were able to determine that the disease was caused by a virus (and that the virus is not partial to any particular lifestyle or gender).

This virus has gone by several different names, which you may have seen in AIDS reports: HTLV-III, LAV, and most recently, HIV— which stands for Human Immunosuppressant Virus. In this book we usually refer to it as "the AIDS virus."

Patrick says that he is puzzled by the new words he hears when AIDS is in the news: **"I read in a pamphlet that AIDS is spread through 'exchange of body fluids,' but I don't understand what body fluids they mean. Are they talking about blood?"**
The body fluids are: blood, semen, vaginal secretions, menstrual flow, saliva, tears, urine, intestinal secretions, and lymph. The AIDS virus is found in these body fluids, especially in blood and semen.

It is transmitted from person to person only through the exchange of these fluids. "Exchange" means when some blood or semen from one person gets into another person's body through the skin or mucous membrane.

The two most common routes by which the virus is passed from an infected person to an unprotected person are unprotected sexual intercourse (with virus-infected semen—and possibly vaginal secretions, saliva, urine, and feces) and shared needles (contaminated with blood).

"What does 'unprotected' sexual intercourse mean?"
Unprotected intercourse means having sex without using mechanical and chemical barriers—like a condom and vaginal foam. When someone has unprotected intercourse with a person who has the AIDS virus,

there is a good chance of becoming infected with the virus—and eventually coming down with AIDS. The carrier may have no symptoms, may appear vigorous and healthy, but still may be carrying the virus in the bloodstream.

"How does IV drug use cause AIDS?"

Infected blood is often transferred on shared needles that are used to shoot up drugs. The amount of blood can be a tiny, almost invisible trace, but may still carry the virus.

Since most people who have the AIDS virus show no symptoms, it is impossible to recognize them. To share a needle, even just once, is to put yourself in deadly danger.

"How can a baby get AIDS?"

A third way that the virus gets passed on is during childbirth. A pregnant woman who is infected with the AIDS virus transmits it to her baby before or during childbirth. The baby's life is usually very short. Mothers who are at risk for AIDS are advised not to breastfeed infants.

"The papers say people get AIDS if they're promiscuous. Is that true?"

The more partners one has, the greater the chance that one of the partners will be infected and will transmit the AIDS virus, especially if barriers like condoms and foam are not used. If a person is already sexually active, it makes sense to limit the number of one's sex partners. Next to abstinence, there is least risk with only one partner— a person who has had no other partners. But even one unsafe, unprotected sexual contact is all that is needed to transmit the virus. A virus cannot distinguish between people who have a great deal of sexual activity and those who have very little.

"Can you get AIDS even if you've just started having sex?"

Anybody can get AIDS at any age. Anybody who engages in risky sexual acts or needle-sharing can acquire the virus. It is the risky behavior, and not the sexual orientation, that puts one at risk. It is a dangerous misconception to think of AIDS as a gay men's disease.

Although the reported heterosexual cases are fewer than the homosexual cases at this time, some medical scientists predict that, at some time in the future, heterosexuals will make up the majority of AIDS cases.

"Can't the spread of AIDS be stopped?"
Medical scientists are seeking a vaccine to prevent AIDS, but there is little expectation of success in the near future. Therefore, education for the prevention of AIDS transmission is the only way to stop the spread of this disease.

"Is AIDS terribly contagious?"
No, AIDS is not classified as a contagious disease, like the flu or a cold. The virus functions only in body fluids like semen and blood. People do not catch it from coughs or sneezes or shaking hands.

"Is there any way of killing the virus?"
Not if it has entered the body. But outside the body it is easily destroyed with common household detergents, bleach, peroxide, or alcohol. It is

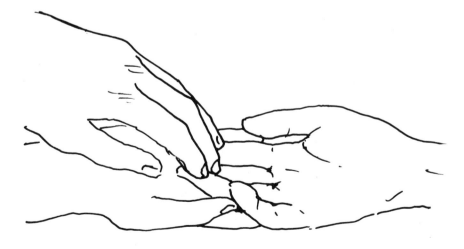

You do *not* get AIDS from:

> Food
>
> Air
>
> Water

You do *not* get AIDS from:

> Toilet seats
>
> Doorknobs
>
> Telephones
>
> Towels
>
> Drinking glasses and dishes
>
> Coughs and sneezes
>
> Insects and animals
>
> Giving blood

You do *not* get AIDS from:

> Holding hands
>
> Touching
>
> Dry kissing
>
> Hugging
>
> Body massage
>
> Caressing
>
> Masturbation
>
> Clothed petting

also destroyed by chemical contraceptives—spermicides such as non-oxynol-9, which is contained in vaginal foam, and in water-soluble spermicidal lubricants such as ForPlay, Lubraceptic, and PrePair.

"How does the AIDS virus get into a person's blood?"

People who have contracted AIDS have allowed the virus in one of the body fluids of an infected person to enter their own bloodstreams through a break in skin or in mucous membrane or in a blood vessel. This is the only way that AIDS can be transmitted.

"Isn't it dangerous to get a blood transfusion?"

You may have read about some people who got the virus through blood transfusions that were given before March 1985. Some are persons with a blood disease called hemophilia; others had required blood during operations, or were accident victims.

The United States Public Health Service reports that today, because of the careful way that donated blood is screened, there is almost no danger of this happening.

"Is it safe to give blood?"

Yes! Since the needles that are used to draw blood from donors are sterile-packaged and never used again, there is absolutely no possibility of getting the virus when donating blood.

"How many people have AIDS now?"

More than 115,000 cases of AIDS have been reported in the United States as of December 1989. About 69,000 of these people have died. Although there may be many unreported cases, it is estimated that about 365,000 cases will have been reported by the end of 1992, and about 263,000 will have died.

The average life expectancy of a person diagnosed with AIDS is about two years, but new medicines are helping to prolong life.

In addition to these, hundreds of thousands of people have a condition called ARC, which stands for AIDS-Related Complex. They are virus-infected and may have a variety of less severe symptoms such as loss of appetite, unexplained weight loss, fever, skin rashes, and swollen lymph nodes.

"I read that millions of people have the AIDS virus, but they're not all sick. Can they infect other people?"

It is estimated that as many as 1.5 million people in the United States have been infected with the virus; most of these people have no symptoms, do not know they are infected, and may unwittingly infect others.

Although they are not sick now, the virus in their bodies may at some future time become active. The active virus can then multiply, seriously weaken the body's defenses, and allow opportunistic diseases to attack. The AIDS diagnosis means that one of these diseases is present.

"Do other countries have AIDS, too?"

AIDS is pandemic—a worldwide epidemic. Estimates for the number of people infected with the AIDS virus in the world range between five million and thirty million. The largest numbers of AIDS cases are in the developing countries, especially in central Africa, where at least one tenth of the population carries the virus. Most cases in Africa have been transmitted heterosexually; women and men contract the disease in equal numbers.

AIDS is spreading in South America, especially in Brazil. And it is widespread on the island of Haiti. In Europe, it is a serious problem in Belgium, Denmark, Switzerland, France, England, and West Germany. In North America, Mexico and Canada also have significant numbers of AIDS cases.

"How do you know if you have AIDS?"

AIDS can be diagnosed only by a doctor, but tests have been developed to check for the presence of the HIV virus that causes AIDS. The tests determine if there are certain antibodies in the bloodstream. Presence of these antibodies shows that the body has reacted to the presence of a foreign substance—the virus. But the tests are not perfect—they sometimes give false results. This is why a second test is required to verify the presence of HIV. Tests cannot check on recent risky exposure because it may take months for the body to develop antibodies to the virus.

These tests show that a person has been infected with the HIV virus, but the disease may not develop for years.

"If you're worried, where can you get tested?"

People who want to know if they have the virus may get tested at a medical clinic. But persons who seek testing must be sure that they will get good pre-test and post-test counseling at the test site since the test results may be emotionally overwhelming. In most cities there are Alternative AIDS Test Sites, where people may be tested anonymously. (Anonymity is important to protect your civil rights.) To find out if there is such a test site in your city, phone the local Board of Health or an AIDS hotline (listed on page 114).

> Helene tells of her sister, who has a special reason for being tested.
>
> "My sister, Millie, has been married to Lloyd for three years now, and both of them are dying to have a baby. The trouble is that when she married him, she had only known Lloyd for about six months. When they got serious, he told her that he used to shoot up but that he had been clean for a couple of years.
>
> "What Millie doesn't want is to infect a baby with AIDS. Neither does Lloyd, but he thinks she's overreacting, and he isn't sure that being tested is a good idea. Well, Millie called an AIDS hotline and found out that they can be tested anonymously. The guy she spoke to on the phone said that the first step would be to speak to a counselor so maybe the trouble they are having about it can be resolved.
>
> "Millie says that if Lloyd refuses to be tested, she won't even consider having a baby."

Whether people test positive or negative, they still must follow the AIDS guidelines. People who test positive (who have the virus) need to follow the protective AIDS guidelines to shield themselves from further infection that could make their own virus more active—and also to protect others.

People who test negative—who have not developed antibodies to the virus—must follow the AIDS guidelines to protect themselves.

The test results cannot show any effects of recent exposure to the virus because it may take even longer than six months for the body to produce the AIDS virus antibodies which mark the presence of the virus.

Some people have become obsessed with the fear of AIDS. Valerie thinks that her only course is to get tested. She says:

"I don't know what to do. I don't take drugs, and I've never dated anyone who does, but I'm scared stiff. I kissed a guy I had just met at a party last month, and then I saw him smoking pot. What if he shoots up, too? Now I'm driving myself crazy. How do I know that he doesn't have AIDS? The only way I'll rest easy is if I take the test."

In this case, where panic has set in, it would be best for Valerie to call an AIDS hotline and describe her fears and worries as frankly as possible. A youth counselor may be recommended, with whom Valerie can discuss her problem.

"How can you tell if you have AIDS?"
The symptoms are the same as for many other illnesses. If they persist week after week, they may be suspicious. Only a doctor can diagnose AIDS.

The symptoms include:

Feeling tired for no apparent reason

Having lost a great deal of weight for no apparent reason

Soaking night sweats

Lumps on the sides of the neck, under the arms, or around the groin

Purplish patches on the skin that don't go away

Watery bowel movements that persist for weeks

But remember that these same symptoms are usually present in common minor illnesses such as colds, stomach flu, or bronchitis. Compared to these illnesses, AIDS is still relatively uncommon.

* * *

The AIDS virus is commonly transmitted through anal or vaginal intercourse. However, barriers such as condoms and foam reduce the risk of transmission. The next chapter will discuss these and other mechanical and chemical barriers.

6

Becoming Responsible About Sexual Intercourse

"I don't want to get AIDS. What should I do so I won't get it?"
The AIDS epidemic is unlike the plagues of the past. It is different in that today we know how we can protect ourselves. In past centuries, when cholera and small pox epidemics were killing off large numbers of people, the rest of the population was helpless. But today we are fortunate in knowing what we can do to reduce our risk of infection.

We can modify our behavior so that there will be no possibility of viral infection resulting from sexual contact—we can practice *abstinence*—refraining from sexual intercourse.

However, we are aware that recommendations of abstinence in the past have had little effect on people's behavior—just as the demonstrated risk of early death from drinking-and-driving or from smoking goes mainly unheeded.

"Is abstinence really the only way I can be safe?"
Yes, abstinence is the safest way, if you are also drug-free. But back in Chapter Three we wrote about the broad range of sexual pleasures that some people enjoy without the risks that come with sexual intercourse and the exchange of body fluids. Exploring these

alternatives may lessen worry while providing for sexual gratification and the lessening of sexual tension.

"If I go on having sex anyway, how can I make it safer?"

This chapter describes the use of multiple barriers as a way of reducing the risks in sexual intercourse. This is important information for those young people who have been "having sex" for years, and do not want to change their established patterns.

Sexual intercourse becomes less risky with *layers of protection*—the mechanical and chemical barriers that have been developed to protect us from sexually transmitted diseases.

But these layers of protection must be used every time there is sexual intercourse, and used correctly, carefully, and skillfully.

For people who are having sexual intercourse the "combination method" of using vaginal foam and the condom at the same time is highly recommended. Partners ideally share responsibility for each other's health, pleasure, and peace of mind. Foam and condom, used correctly, provide maximum protection.

Barriers to the AIDS virus:

> Condoms
> Vaginal foam
> Contraceptive suppositories and tablets
> Contraceptive sponge
> Diaphragm with spermicidal gel or cream
> Water-base lubricant containing nonoxynol-9
> Dental dams
> Latex gloves

In the following pages of this chapter the list of protective barriers will be described individually. But first, let us talk about the objections.

"It seems so embarrassing—so gross—to make all these preparations. Isn't making love supposed to be spontaneous?"

"Spontaneity" is no longer a reasonable ideal, especially with the dangers that the AIDS virus presents today. But in the days when young people could choose to be spontaneous about sexual intercourse, the few moments of spontaneity were almost always followed by worry and guilt.

To label life-preserving preparations as "gross" seems to be a way of trying to avoid embarrassment at any cost. The costs, however, are too high. Giving embarrassment that kind of power over your life is unfair to yourself.

THE CONTRACEPTIVE FOR MEN: The Condom (or Rubber)

"How old do you have to be to buy a condom?"
Condoms are sold to persons of any age. It is best to get them at a drugstore or clinic. Condoms are also sold by mail order and in vending machines. Mike, who is sixteen, says:

> "It's too hard for me to just go into a store and ask for rubbers because I'm really self-conscious. I don't want everybody looking at me and seeing me sweat."

Many people are uncomfortably self-conscious and even dread the first experience of asking a clerk for contraceptives. But the embarrassment is quickly over, and the next purchase is usually easier.

Many drugstores are now displaying condoms on their racks, close to the pharmacist's counter, so that customers can make their selections more comfortably. Some drugstores now display condoms in the feminine hygiene sections, because stores have found that 40 percent of their condom sales are now made to women.

"I wouldn't be too embarrassed to buy some rubbers at a drugstore in another neighborhood, but I don't think I could take it out when I'm making out with somebody. I'm afraid I could lose my hard-on just trying to open the package and get it on me. Is there a trick to staying hard?"
No, for some who may have neglected to practice when they are alone,

it is at first an impossible feat. Some young men have found that it helps to turn it into a cooperative enterprise, with the partner opening the package and rolling the condom onto the penis.

Bill, who is seventeen, has bought condoms at a drugstore because Julie and he have been tempted to go all the way. Bill says:

"I've bought them, but how can I tell Julie—straight out like that, 'I want to have sex with you with a rubber.' She'll think I've planned it, and she might get mad.

"Sometimes we're necking in the car, and we're going at it pretty hot and heavy, and I'm dying to say, 'Hey, I've got a condom. Let's do it tonight!' But I get scared about her reaction."

Instead of pretending that the sex act is a spontaneous one that requires no preparation or planning, it would be wiser, in spite of the awkward feeling, to discuss with your partner what you both would like.

In addition, if you decide that you both want sexual intercourse, it is best to share the responsibility and preparations: both partners need their own "layers of protection"—foam for the female, condom for the male.

"But don't rubbers reduce sensation?"

Not necessarily and not significantly. This concern about reduced sensation is usually expressed by young men who have not yet used condoms. Condoms are now available that are incredibly thin, yet tough. But it is a good idea to masturbate with a condom first to get used to the feeling and to get accustomed to handling it. You may even find that the condom gives you better control of the timing of your orgasm.

Some men have found that by using a couple of drops of a water-soluble lubricant containing nonoxynol-9 *inside* the tip of the condom, the sensation and pleasurable feeling is increased for the man. At the same time the nonoxynol-9 adds an important safety factor.

Josh, who is sixteen, says:

"It was a big day for me when I finally got up the nerve to buy a condom. Actually I bought three—in case I tore one. But then I figured I'd better learn how to get it on before I tried to have sex with anyone.

"I unrolled it and then tried to pull it onto my penis, but it didn't work that way. Then I looked at the directions that came in the package, and I realized that I had to roll it up and try again, unrolling it onto my hard-on. I did get it on and then I jacked off, imagining I was fooling around with a girl I know.

"Then I pulled off the rubber with the cum inside, and I felt great—as if I had really accomplished something.

"I still haven't tried to make it with a girl, and I don't know when I will, but at least I'll know how to handle the rubber mechanics when I do make it."

"I see so many different brands. How do I know which brand to buy? Are there different sizes?"

There are minor size differences, but since condoms stretch to fit, size is not usually an important consideration for most men. However, penis lengths do vary. Condom lengths vary from 7-1/8 inches to 8-5/8 inches.

"What's the safest kind of condom to use?"

Most condoms are made of latex—a kind of thin, tough, elastic rubber. Latex is the safest material. Condoms made of lambskin are also available for the very few who are allergic to latex.

There are other important differences to learn about. Some brands are lubricated with nonoxynol-9, a spermicide that helps protect against sexually transmitted diseases, including AIDS, and against unwanted pregnancy. They cost no more than other brands, and should be the first choice.

However, some people have minor allergic reactions to non-oxynol-9—they experience itching after use. These people may want to use one of the brands lubricated with gel or silicone. Though not a chemical barrier, the lubricant adds an important safety factor—there is less likelihood of the condom's tearing because of dry friction.

"Are all brands lubricated?"

No, a third type is packaged dry, without lubrication. The usual choice for oral sex (fellatio) is one of these unlubricated condoms. However, if you use a dry condom for intercourse, you should apply a water-soluble lubricant like K-Y Jelly or Ramses Spermicidal Lubricant.

"I've seen lots of condom brands that claim to have better texture or shape. Is that important?"

Variations in shape and texture are relatively unimportant. Most condoms come with nipple-shaped reservoir tips (to catch the semen), and some are plain-tipped; some are textured in various ways, and some are smooth; some are incredibly thin, and a few brands are thick

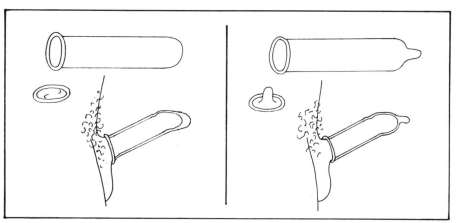

Some condoms have receptacle (or reservoir) tips to catch the semen at ejaculation. Others have blunt ends. If you use the plain-ended condoms, do not stretch the condom tightly against the head of the penis, but leave about a half-inch space at the end for the semen. This helps prevent semen from seeping out along the shaft of the penis. When unrolling the condom onto the penis, hold the tip closed, so that air won't get trapped in the tip. Unroll the condom all the way down to the base of the penis.

After sex, hold the condom around the base to be sure no semen drips out near the female genitals, and withdraw the penis carefully.

and tough. They come in white, black, and in vivid or pastel colors; some are transparent, and some are opaque.

"My older brother uses a kind of special condom that costs a lot. Is it really better?"

There is one new type available—the expensive Mentor condom, priced at about $1.75 each (in boxes of six), which seems to be an improvement in risk-reduction design. It has an adhesive to keep it clinging to the penis after loss of erection. This is important because it is probable that most condom failures result from seeping of semen down the penis shaft while withdrawing the penis after intercourse. (The failures are in user technique—incorrect handling of the condom after ejaculation.)

Young men who buy and use condoms find that they like some brands better than others—condom users develop personal preferences. Pricing of condoms, except in the case of Mentor, does not seem to be related to quality.

"I read that you have to test condoms. Do you blow them up?"

No. Since condoms come pre-tested it is not necessary for the user to test them—in fact it is dangerous to test them yourself because they may be damaged in the process.

All condoms manufactured in the United States must meet government standards for reliability. Japanese-made condoms seem just as reliable. All manufacturers have systematic testing programs.

"Is the condom really reliable?"

Reliability depends mostly on how correctly it is used and then how carefully it is taken off the penis after use.

Condoms usually come rolled up and individually sealed in a plastic or aluminum package. The package must be opened carefully to avoid tearing the condom. Condoms are surprisingly tough, but they can be torn by accident with a jagged fingernail.

Before unrolling onto the penis, half an inch of the tip of the condom is squeezed so that air does not get trapped in the end. The tip is held closed as the condom is unrolled onto the erect penis. If the penis is uncircumcised, the foreskin should be pushed back before drawing on the condom.

"Can the condom just be unrolled over the head of the penis?"
The condom must be rolled *all the way* up the shaft of the penis so that semen cannot seep out along the shaft. It should always be put on before the penis is anywhere near the vulva (or the entrance to the vagina). If the condom is put on before the penis has become erect, it should be rolled up to the base as the penis hardens.

John, who is a senior in Manhattan, describes a risky situation:

"My best friend told me that after he had sex with his girl friend, using protection, they fell asleep. When he woke up, he saw that he didn't have the condom on. It was still in the girl. He's not worried, but I know I would be."

"How are you supposed to take off a condom?"
After ejaculation, withdrawal should be immediate, before losing the erection. Many pregnancies occur because of failure to remove the condom correctly. To prevent semen from seeping out near the vagina, the condom is held by the rim against the base of the penis while the penis is withdrawn. And never attempt to use the same condom more than once.

The condom can be considered a "first line of defense." When a condom is used, it lessens the risk of transmitting STDs, including the AIDS virus, and helps protect against an unwanted pregnancy. But how effective it is depends mostly on how carefully it is used and also how consistently. The condom must be used *every single time* there is penetration sex.

LUBRICANTS

Although most condoms come prelubricated with a film of water-soluble lubricant, with prolonged intercourse the condom tends to dry out in spots; then tearing is possible. Therefore it is helpful to use an additional water-soluble lubricant (like Ramses Spermicidal Lubricant, K-Y Jelly, or a vaginal contraceptive gel or cream) on the condom after rolling it up on the penis, and also on the vagina.

Some of these lubricants contain a spermicide which increases their protective function. A spermicidal lubricant prevents the sperm from fertilizing the egg, while helping to protect both partners from infection.

A word of caution: Drugstores display both types of lubricant on the same shelves. Therefore it is necessary to read labels carefully.

Another way to make condom use more effective is to put a couple of drops of spermicidal lubricant inside the tip of the condom before unrolling it onto the penis. In addition to the increased safety, the

HOW TO USE A CONDOM: EFFECTIVENESS DEPENDS ON PROPER USE

Open carefully, avoid tearing the condom.

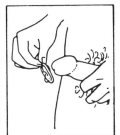

Place against penis, preferably when erect.

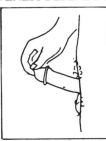

Hold condom tip closed to avoid trapping air.

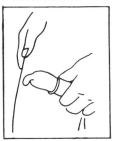

Unroll the condom onto penis.

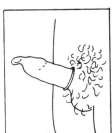

Condom should cover entire penis length.

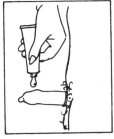

Put extra water-base lubricant on the condom.

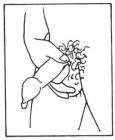

After sex, hold rim tightly, withdraw penis.

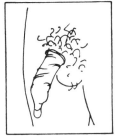

Discard; do not use a condom more than one time.

slipperiness around the head of the penis increases the male's sensation. At least one brand, Lifestyles Extra Strength Gold Pack, is sold with spermicide within the tip, in addition to spermicidal lubricant on the outside.

"I hear guys talk about Vaseline for sex. Is it OK to use it?"
Never use any oil-base lubricant—like baby oil, vegetable shortening, cold cream, Vaseline or other petroleum products—with rubber. It can cause the latex to deteriorate and tear. In addition, if oils get into body openings (vagina or rectum), they make it difficult for the body's natural self-cleansing secretions to function.

SAFER SEXUAL INTERCOURSE: Choices For Women

"Isn't it enough if my boyfriend uses a rubber?"
No, it is safer to use layers of protection. The female should use a contraceptive, too. It makes sense for each person to become responsible for her or his own safety.

Occasionally the condom fails. The usual cause is unskilled or careless use. It may have spent years deteriorating in someone's pocket or in the hot glove compartment of a car. Never keep condoms in a glove compartment—it gets too hot for the latex. If it has been carried in a wallet or pants pocket, it should be replaced with a fresh one after a few months. Accidents do happen.

Maggie is worried about how contraceptives may affect her ability to have an orgasm: **"I started having sex with my boyfriend and we use condoms and foam but he doesn't give me an orgasm at all. Could that be on account of the birth control or because he's inexperienced or he's undersexed or am I too screwed up about sex?"**
None of the above. The female's stimulation does not seem to be affected by contraceptives. Males are not magically endowed with the ability to "give" orgasms to females. People who want to experience orgasm usually learn how, when alone, through trial and error.

Since there is no correct level of sexiness and we are all differently built and conditioned, no one can be "undersexed" or "oversexed." And no, no one can be too screwed up. Everyone is a little confused about sex, and fortunately, with a little information (or a lot of it), almost everyone can work out an enjoyable sex life.

"I read these romances where they start having sex and the man makes the woman come. Isn't that how it's supposed to be?"

In romance fiction, when men and women have intercourse, the woman comes automatically and is grateful to the man. In real life only about 50 percent of women having intercourse experience orgasm—some of the time. Therefore, it is not a response that can be expected just to happen. It does just happen for some—for others, it takes learning.

Many women who engage in masturbation or petting do have orgasms. Usually the orgasm comes about in some specific position with specific stimulating strokes at specific spots on the body. If just that combination is transferred to the intercourse situation, orgasm may result, but not necessarily.

VAGINAL FOAM

"What's the safest protection for a woman?"

For women, foam seems to be the best choice for protection from AIDS and other sexually transmitted diseases, and also from unplanned pregnancy. It is effective, inexpensive, and easy to get at the drugstore without a prescription.

Foam is a medicated mixture that comes in a small aerosol can and is placed in the vagina by means of an applicator. Foam spreads into crevices and forms a mechanical barrier to block the sperm from entering the cervix while a safe chemical (nonoxynol-9) stops the sperm's forward movement. It coats the vaginal walls more evenly than any of the other chemical contraceptives, so that disease germs cannot get through them.

Alice, who is planning to go to college and then to become a lawyer, has been looking at the feminine hygiene displays at the drugstore.

"I've been reading about Safe Sex and 'layers of protection.' My boyfriend and I do fool around a lot, although we don't go all the way, except once when we got carried away—but he pulled out in time. I trust him, but I think he's had lots of other girlfriends before me. I don't want to get AIDS or STD or get pregnant, so I realized that I better buy some foam and use it in case we get carried away again.

"The drugstore had it on display with contraceptive sponges and douches and tampons, and I just picked up the foam package and brought it to the counter. The girl took my money and put it in a bag, and if I was blushing or looking nervous, she didn't seem to notice at all.

"It took me a couple of days to try it, but finally I did, and it was okay. When I saw Tom, my boyfriend, I told him about the foam, and then I said I wanted him to get condoms.

"At first he said, 'Why? we're not going all the way.' But I reminded him of our narrow escape, and he really listened."

INSERTING VAGINAL FOAM

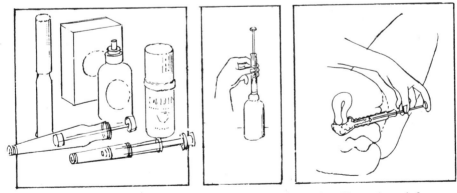

Put two full applicators of foam deep into the vagina, no more than fifteen minutes before intercourse. If more than fifteen minutes have gone by without starting intercourse, put in another applicator of foam.

Foam provides a double barrier: It works two ways. It is both a mechanical barrier and a safe chemical barrier—forming an effective partnership with the condom. Containing a high concentration of nonoxynol-9, it is the most effective of the chemical contraceptives.

Several brands are widely available. If they are not on display at the drugstore, ask for them by name. Delfen, Emko, Because, and Koromex Foam come in "starter" packages with plastic applicator included. Refills are sold without applicator, so it's necessary to buy the package with the applicator when foam is used for the first time. Each use comes out to between thirty cents and one dollar. Some of the packages are small enough to carry in pocket or purse.

Foam is a convenient method of protection. No medical exam or prescription is needed to buy vaginal foam—it is displayed in drugstores and supermarkets near the sanitary napkins. Anyone can buy foam—there are no legal age restrictions. Family planning clinics provide foam, too, at reduced cost, or even free for people who have no income.

"Is foam really safe?"

There are no health risks or medical side effects that result from the use of foam. The active ingredient in foam, nonoxynol-9, has been used in foods and feminine hygiene products for years. If some people find that they have an allergic reaction to a foam product, switching to another brand is advised. The discomfort of the allergic reaction is usually brief.

"Is it safe enough to use foam by itself?"

No, it is not. Foam is a first-rate partner to the condom, but it does not furnish adequate protection when used alone.

How foam is used: It is easy to insert; directions will be found on the package. They suggest shaking the container well (at least twenty times) in order to make the mixture bubble. It is best to put two full applicators of foam deep into the vagina no more than fifteen minutes before sexual intercourse—the closer to intercourse, the better. If there is a second round of sex, it is necessary to put more foam into the vagina, even if the second act is only a few minutes after the first.

One must never douche immediately after the sex act because that would destroy the foam's effectiveness. If you must douche, wait for at least six hours.

FOAMING SUPPOSITORIES AND TABLETS

Another convenient form in which chemical contraceptives are made is the vaginal insert. These are small solid ovals or bullet shapes that are inserted deep into the vagina (with the finger). Body heat causes them to melt and foam. It is necessary to wait about fifteen minutes (but not more than thirty minutes) before having intercourse. If there is a second act of intercourse, a new suppository must be inserted.

The instructions that come in the package should be studied before the contraceptive is used with a partner. It is a good idea to try it out first when alone, so that its use with a partner will be more comfortable.

These devices, too, are perfectly safe, with no health risks or medical side effects.

INSERTING VAGINAL SUPPOSITORY

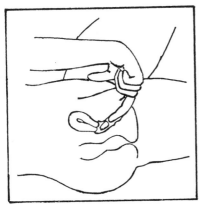 

After inserting—deep into the vagina—wait fifteen minutes before having intercourse. If more than thirty minutes go by without intercourse, insert another suppository or foaming tablet.

THE VAGINAL CONTRACEPTIVE SPONGE

"I see lots of ads for the Today Sponge. Is there any advantage over foam?"

Some women like the fact that the Today Contraceptive Sponge may be left in place (in the vagina, against the cervix) for as long as twenty-four hours. However, it must be left in the vagina for six hours after the last act of intercourse.

The Contraceptive Sponge combines the advantages of mechanical and chemical (nonoxynol-9) barriers. Like the condom and foam, it can be bought at any drugstore without a doctor's prescription. It is effective in partnership with the condom.

The Contraceptive Sponge, like the condom, can be used only once and is then discarded.

THE DIAPHRAGM

"I thought the diaphragm was supposed to be the best protection."
The diaphragm is effective in reducing the risk of unplanned pregnancy, but only the cervix and reproductive organs are protected from AIDS and other STDs; the vulva and vagina remain vulnerable. For least risk, it should be used with the condom.

The diaphragm is a small, bowl-shaped soft rubber cap with a

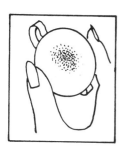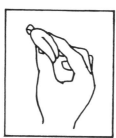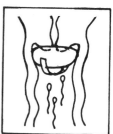

Detailed instructions come packaged with the contraceptive sponge. They should be followed carefully. Once the sponge is inserted there is no need to wait to have intercourse, which may be repeated within a twenty-four-hour period without further preparation. But the sponge must be left in place at least six hours after the last act of intercourse.

flexible springy rim. It must be prescribed by a doctor and fitted by a doctor or nurse. This can be done at clinics such as Planned Parenthood, where fees are usually based on what the client can afford.

Before using it, the woman spreads at least a teaspoonful of spermicidal gel or cream on the inside surface and also along the rim. The diaphragm must be used every single time that you have intercourse. It must be left in the vagina for six to eight hours after the last intercourse.

Equal responsibility: When today's young woman has decided that she is ready for sexual intercourse, she can no longer rely on her partner to provide the necessary protection. Nor can her partner rely on her. Young people must take responsibility for their own health and survival!

HOW TO INSERT THE DIAPHRAGM, PLACE IT IN POSITION, AND REMOVE IT

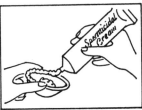

Spread at least a tea-spoon of contraceptive gel or cream inside the diaphragm, around rim.

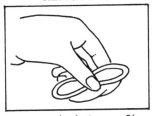

Squeeze rim between fin-gers so that it folds in half. Insert as you would a tampon.

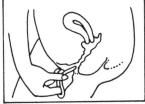

Push as far back as it will go. Then let go and it will open up to cover the cervix.

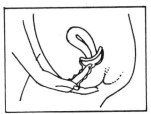

Tuck front rim of the diaphragm behind the pubic bone. Touch the cervix through rubber to make sure that it is covered completely.

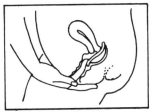

To remove diaphragm (at least six hours after last act of intercourse). Hook your finger over the top of the rim to break the suction.

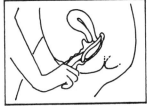

Then pull the diaphragm down and out. It should never be left in place longer than 24 hours, which could result in the growth of bacteria.

THE NEW VAGINAL CONDOM

A type of condom that a female can insert in the vagina has been designed and tested and may soon be available in drugstores. It does not require fitting by a doctor or nurse, and in addition to protecting the vagina from infection, it protects the labia and the base of the penis.

"Is oral sex a safe thing to do?"

Oral/genital sex may be risky unless a mechanical barrier such as a dental dam (for cunnilingus—stimulating the female genitals with the tongue) or a condom (for fellatio—mouth stimulation of the penis) is used. These latex barriers are suggested because STD infections occur in the mouth as well as in the genitals and anus, and can be passed from mouth to genitals or from genitals to mouth.

The dental dam is a small square of latex that dentists use for isolating a tooth preparatory to working on it. It may be placed on the vulva for oral sex, as a barrier between tongue and genitals. Dental dams may be bought in surgical supply stores and in some drugstores. Nonlubricated condoms are usually preferred for fellatio.

The high-risk practice of oral/anal sex ("rimming") often results in transmission of intestinal parasites and other diseases which undermine the health. If, in spite of the great risk, oral-anal sex continues to be practiced, it can be made less risky with the use of a dental dam.

"I thought they only do anal sex in the videos. Why is anal sex considered so risky?"

Anal intercourse is believed to have been the most common route of AIDS virus transmission in the first years of the disease spread in the United States. Therefore, many people have given up anal sex.

However, if this high-risk behavior is practiced, a condom must always be used to protect both partners. Stronger condoms labeled "Extra Strength" are the best choice. Condoms may be doubled, one over the other. Generous use of a water-base lubricant is also necessary, and a couple of drops of nonoxynol-9 should be placed within the tip of the condom.

"What if you have a cut or open sore on your hand, and you're starting to make out? Could you get an infection that way?"
Contact with semen, blood, or menstrual flow may put you at risk if you have scratches or cuts on your fingers and you are engaged in genital petting with a new partner. Hangnails are common and may be a port of entry. A virus carried in the partner's body fluid can enter your blood stream through a cut or break in the skin.

Disposable *latex or plastic gloves* like the ones used by physicians and dentists greatly increase your safety. They are sold in drugstores and supermarkets.

However, ordinary everyday contacts such as shaking hands, hugging, and dry kissing present no risk to the healthy person.

* * *

Keeping the body in good health. If you are having sex: In addition to using Safe Sex barriers it is important to keep your body as healthy as possible, because a body weakened by drugs, alcohol, or disease is more easily attacked by the AIDS virus. The next chapter will discuss the relationship between substance abuse, poor nutrition, STDs, and AIDS.

7

Substance Abuse and Abuse of the Body

Annie, a high school sophomore, asks: **"If AIDS is a sex disease, how come people on drugs are getting it?"**

Sharing a needle (or syringe, bulb, works, or cooker) is the most direct way that the AIDS virus gets transmitted from one body to another. A tiny amount of infected blood remains in the "works" even though you don't see it. Rinsing with water or wiping it dry is not enough—water does not kill the virus.

As a result of this dangerous needle-sharing practice, by November 1989 about 32,000 AIDS cases among IV drug users had been reported, and more than 18,000 of these people have already died. Besides these reported cases, medical scientists believe that there are many that have not been diagnosed.

"There's no way I can get new needles and I'm not about to stop doing drugs. What do I do?"

First, call the AIDS Hotline, 1-800-342-AIDS, toll-free. Another source of drug information is 1-800-522-5353. Your state or city health department, listed in the local phone book, may suggest a local referral.

Second, reduce your risk of infection by cleaning your works correctly. *Ordinary household bleach* is recommended for cleaning works before use; it is the simplest, easiest, cheapest method. Mix three tablespoons of bleach in a cup of water. Draw the liquid up the syringe, shake well, squirt it out. Repeat a second time. Then fill syringe with plain *tap water* to get rid of the bleach, shake, squirt it out. Repeat with water. Any water you use must be clean, unused by anyone else. If new works are bought on the street, they must be cleaned this way, too.

"Is there any risk in getting a tattoo?"

Skin puncturing with any shared needle—for any purpose—can allow the virus to enter the bloodstream. This category includes "skin-popping," shared tattoo needles, ear-piercing needles, or needles and pins used in piercing other parts of the body. Needles used in acupuncture treatments must be properly sterilized before use.

Areas of heavy drug use: In some cities *most* AIDS cases result from sharing of needles. It has been reported that 80 percent of the AIDS cases in Newark, New Jersey, are IV drug users.

Large numbers of drug-related AIDS cases have been reported, too, in New York, Los Angeles, San Francisco, and Miami. In New York, more than 65 percent of IV drug users are believed to be AIDS virus infected.

"I saw a magazine article that said more women are getting AIDS nowadays. Is that true?"

More and more women are now at risk. As many as one-third of women who have AIDS have caught the disease from sexual contact with IV drug users who had become infected by sharing needles.

"Do prostitutes get AIDS because they are promiscuous?"

Many prostitutes, both female and male, are IV drug users or used to be, or have sex partners who share needles. They are therefore at very high risk for getting the AIDS virus.

Although some prostitutes have been using condoms and mouth

germicides, some, for a fee, are persuaded by clients to have intercourse without a condom. Therefore, it is foolhardy to have any kind of unprotected penetration sex with anyone who exchanges sex for cash—whether professionally or just on occasion.

"I don't shoot up. All I do is I use uppers and downers. My mother is always after me because I guess I skip a lot of meals. She's worried about AIDS—should I be?"

The use of alcohol and other drugs causes serious health problems. Malnutrition is common among heavy users of these substances. Amphetamines (speed), marijuana, amyl and butyl nitrites (poppers), and alcohol all damage the body's immune system and make it easier for the AIDS virus to attack. Weakened defenses make the body an easy target for "opportunistic diseases."

"But doesn't everybody drink? I like to get high before I make out. I'd be too nervous if I tried to get it on with a girl without a couple of drinks first. I might not get it up and the news would get around fast."

No, not everyone drinks, although it sometimes seems that way. Some people get nervous about sex because they realize that they do not know much about it, and they worry that their lack of knowledge will be obvious to others. The thing to do is to get information, and with it, confidence.

Concern about lack of erection is common, especially for young men who are judging their performance. It helps to think of sexual contact as a way to express affection and to have pleasure rather than as a command performance. Almost every male finds himself at times in situations where he cannot "get it up." It may mean that he is not really interested in being sexual at that time—or that he is uncomfortable, or tired, or has had too much alcohol.

"I don't get drunk on a couple of beers. How can just a few drinks put anyone at risk?"

Alcohol and other drugs distort our judgment. Our resolve may melt away; we feel free of cares and we take foolish risks. Maxine testifies to that:

> "Everything I was reading in the papers made me come to a decision. I decided on abstinence—that meant no fooling around. I even gave up kissing. For three months, I abstained from everything.
>
> "Then one night when I was at the bowling alley with my girlfriend, I met this nice-looking guy. He offered to drive us both home, and after we dropped my friend off, we sat in his car and had a few beers. I guess I drank more than I realized.
>
> "When he wanted to have sex, I said, 'Okay.' The next day I felt awful. What a stupid thing to have done! I'll never do anything like that again. It's back to abstinence for me, but this time I'll really have will power."

Maxine may think that "will power" will now serve her better, but what she does not realize is that once she is under the influence of alcohol, neither her mind nor her will are her own.

"I'm usually too scared about the clap or herpes to want to have sex with anybody, but when I'm at a party and I get a little high, I'm OK and I forget about my worries and I can get it on with anybody. How can you tell who has VD?"

There is no way to spot a sexually transmitted disease except to look carefully at a partner's body for signs of disease and to talk openly and honestly with each other about your sex lives. But you are not likely to do either when you are high at a party. In any case, "anybody" is not a safe choice. You had better get to know a person well before choosing him or her as a sex partner.

When you are "stoned," you cannot think straight, and you take risks that endanger your life. You do things that you would never dream of doing in a sober state.

Using alcohol or other drugs to try to "enhance" your sexual experience has become too dangerous in the Age of AIDS. You are better off relying on your imagination and your resourcefulness.

If you want to stay alive and well into your twenties and beyond, you need to have the facts about AIDS and other STDs, alcohol and other drugs, and sex, and you need to be able to make sensible decisions. Safe Sex requires a clear head and intelligent planning.

It is not sensible to give up *all* pleasures, as Maxine attempted, because then we tend to feel sorry for ourselves and eventually have an impulsive fling at high-risk sex, followed by worry and remorse.

Reducing dependency: If you are drinking much or using drugs, it is wise now to consider cutting down or quitting. But people who have already made drugs or alcohol an important part of their lives may find it impossible to give them up without help. There are many substance abuse programs that can help them overcome substance dependency. (See Where to Get Help and Information, pp. 114-115.)

"I don't use drugs. When I want quick energy, I eat a candy bar or grab a Coke. Then I feel great. But after a while I get depressed and nervous. Why?"

The sugar and caffeine in chocolate-covered candy bars and Coke raise your blood sugar rapidly. This rise makes you feel energetic and good—but the sudden energy and good feeling are only temporary.

After the initial rise, the blood sugar begins to drop as rapidly as it rose. What happens now often leads to a feeling of fatigue, depression, and irritability. To feel good again, you may eat another candy bar or have a Coke or a cup of coffee. Then the vicious cycle starts all over again. Such a "quick fix" pattern undermines one's health because it deprives the body of its needed nutrients.

A diet of candy, Coke, and junk food causes malnutrition. When people rely on sugar, starch, and fats for quick energy, they fail to eat nutritious foods, because the empty calories satisfy their hunger. As a result, their bodies do not get the food elements that are essential for growth and good health.

Nutrition research tells us that a diet rich in vegetables, fruits, whole grains, fish, chicken, beans, seeds, and nuts will, in the long run, give us the most energy. A nutritious diet, too, helps to keep our immune system functioning well, so that we are less susceptible to disease.

"I read in a health magazine that if you take certain vitamin pills and minerals like zinc, you strengthen the immune system, and you are protected from AIDS."

Although vitamins and minerals in foods do help to keep us healthy, no amounts of these nutrients can protect us from the AIDS virus once we allow it into our bloodstream (via sexual contact or shared needles). But it is important for us to get a generous variety of vitamins and minerals, and the best way is by eating a variety of unprocessed foods, like those listed above, which contain all the nutrients we need.

"What does health have to do with catching AIDS?"

Poor health habits make the body more vulnerable to AIDS and other disease by weakening its defenses—by sabotaging the production and functioning of the body's white blood cell "soldiers" that are needed to counterattack germ invasion.

Another health safeguard: Exercise is an enjoyable way of keeping our bodies fit—in good shape and resistant to disease. Walking, running, jogging, swimming, cycling, and team sports—practiced regularly—all strengthen the heart, lower the blood pressure, increase our stamina, and provide a feeling of well being.

A good night's sleep is a dividend that rewards people who exercise regularly. In the teen years this is especially important because it is a time of rapid growth and new stresses. Adequate sleep helps to maintain a healthy immune system. Eight hours or so of restful sleep readies the body and mind for the day ahead and keeps us on an even keel.

"What do STDs have to do with getting AIDS?"

Until recently people were careless about protecting themselves from STDs because they believed them easy to cure. The AIDS epidemic requires a change in thinking and behavior.

An STD, even if cured, may leave the reproductive organs scarred and the body more vulnerable to the AIDS virus. The body tissues that are damaged by STDs may allow the AIDS virus or other germs to gain a foothold. Most important, STDs weaken the immune system, so that the body cannot defend itself against the "opportunistic disease" that attacks the immune-deficient body.

For this reason Safe Sex practices are necessary today even if there is little expectation of contact with anyone infected with the AIDS virus.

* * *

Know the STDs. To protect yourself, you need to become familiar with the symptoms and signs of the common sexually transmitted diseases. The next chapter describes them.

8

Facts About the Common STDs

"What's the difference between VD and STDs?"
The initials STD stand for the words Sexually Transmitted Disease. Some of these diseases—gonorrhea and syphilis—were formerly called venereal diseases or VD, and the two names are used interchangeably. Now we know that there are, in addition to gonorrhea and syphilis, many common sexually transmitted diseases.

STDs are infections that spread from one person to another through intimate physical contact—especially sexual intercourse, including oral and anal contacts. They usually infect the sexual and reproductive organs, and also the anus and intestinal tract, as well as the mouth and throat.

STD germs thrive in warm, moist areas like the vagina and vulva, the urethra and prostate, rectum, and mouth.

"My friend had a brown sore on his lip. He took vitamins, and it went away. Was this an STD?"
Only a medical examination would determine whether the lip sore was caused by an STD. Vitamins do not affect STDs; it was just coincidence that the vitamins were taken just as the sore was about to

go away. The sore, the visible sign of an infection, would have disappeared with or without the vitamins—but if the infection was an STD, it was not cured. It went into another stage of the disease.

It seems natural to wait (and worry) when we have STD symptoms, and just hope that they will go away without medical treatment. Sometimes they do, and we believe that we are cured. But the chances are that the infection—if an STD—has gone underground and can continue to damage the body, can easily be transmitted to a partner, and is now harder for a physician to diagnose. Sexually transmitted diseases *must* be treated by a doctor.

"My girlfriend's doctor told her she has 'trich.' He gave her medicine and a prescription for me. I feel fine—why should I take any medicine?"
It is necessary for both partners to be treated—whether or not they have symptoms—to avoid reinfecting each other. Most men who have been infected with trichomoniasis ("trich") are free of symptoms but can still infect a partner.

The rule for STDs is that any partners of an infected person must go for medical treatment so that the cycle of reinfection may be stopped.

Anyone who is twelve or older can be examined and treated without parents' knowledge or permission. The law requires that information about treatment be kept confidential. Clinics respect the teenagers' need for confidentiality.

"I don't even make out yet. Why should I have to learn about this depressing stuff?"
The best time to learn about sexually transmitted diseases is before becoming sexually active. Knowing something about the individual STDs can be helpful in avoiding them or in dealing with them if the need arises.

"I don't know anybody who has an STD. Are STDs all that common?"

STDs are epidemic among the middle teens and older teens. Teenagers and young adults account for most cases.

Each year more than ten million people in the United States become infected with an STD. There may be many additional undisclosed cases because people with sexually transmitted diseases tend to be secretive about them.

An epidemic of silence: Although some STDs are not much harder to pick up than a common cold, many young people think that to contract an STD is somehow shameful. Fear of embarrassment keeps them from seeking medical care or revealing their condition to their partners. If you get an STD, it simply means that you have made some mistake in your sexual behavior. You have done something risky and as a result have picked up one of the STD bugs. The next step is to get immediate medical help. Feeling embarrassed or ashamed or guilty will not get rid of the disease. The best thing to do is to set aside any thoughts of shame—and get to a physician or clinic as quickly as possible.

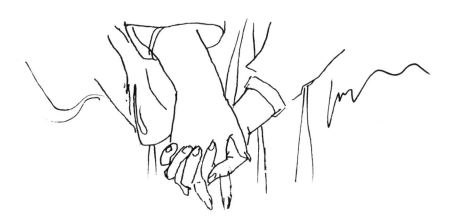

"I've heard of syph, clap, and herpes. Are there other STDs?"

Other common sexually transmitted diseases and conditions are

    Chlamydia

    PID (Pelvic Inflammatory Disease)

    Vaginitis

    NGU (Nongonococcal Urethritis)

    Genital Warts

    Crabs (pubic lice)

    Hepatitis B

—and there are at least another dozen less common ones.

"How can you tell if you have an STD? What are the symptoms?"

If you are female:

- Unusual vaginal discharge or smell
- Itching or burning around vagina
- Vaginal bleeding (when it is not your regular period)
- Pain deep in the vagina during sexual intercourse
- Pain in the belly, above pelvic area

If you are male:

- Discharge or drip from the penis
- Low abdominal (belly) pain

These symptoms occur in both men and women:

- Pain or burning when you urinate or have a bowel movement
- Swelling in the groin, near the sex organs
- Blisters, bumps, or sores, in the mouth or on or near the sex organs or anus
- Redness or swelling in the throat
- Fever, aches, chills

But remember that you may have an STD without any symptoms or signs. If you have had sexual contact with someone who you think may be infected, get a medical examination as soon as possible.

Go to an STD clinic or to a private doctor immediately. It is tempting to delay and hope that "it will go away." Don't put off getting help. Delay is dangerous.

CHLAMYDIA (kla-MID-ea)

Lorna learned about chlamydia in an unfortunate way:

"I never expected to get pregnant because Phil always withdrew. I didn't get my period for a couple of months, but that didn't worry me because I was always pretty irregular. Then one night I got these terrible pains, and my mother and dad rushed me to the emergency room.

"I was stunned when the doctor told me I was pregnant, but not the right way. It was in my tube—the doctor called it an ectopic pregnancy, and I needed surgery. One of my tubes was removed.

"When it was all over and I saw the doctor in his office, he told me about chlamydia. It doesn't always produce symptoms, he said, but I probably had it and it scarred my tubes so that the egg couldn't pass through to the uterus."

The most widespread of the STDs, chlamydia affects about four million Americans each year. The chlamydial infection is spread through sexual intercourse. Most infected women have no symptoms; many infected men are also symptom free. Symptoms, when present, include painful urination, pelvic pain, vaginal discharge, and drip from penis.

Since most infected men and women are unaware that they are infectious, although chlamydia may be silently eroding their reproductive organs, they unwittingly spread the disease.

When neglected, chlamydia can cause scarring of the fallopian tubes, which leads to dangerous ectopic pregnancies (in which the embryo develops outside the uterus, usually in one of the fallopian tubes). It can also cause PID (Pelvic Inflammatory Disease) and sterility.

In men it may cause NGU (nongonococcal urethritis) and infection of the prostate and epididymis (the organ attached to the upper part of the testicle, involved in development of sperm).

99

A baby born to a mother with chlamydia is in danger of being infected during the birth process. This infection may cause blindness or pneumonia, which is often fatal.

GONORRHEA (gon-a-RE-a)

"If my boyfriend has the clap should I go to a doctor even if I feel all right?"

Yes, without question, you must see a physician. Eighty percent of infected women have no symptoms, and men, too, may be symptom free. As with many other STDs, gonorrhea ("the clap") is frequently spread unknowingly.

The symptoms of gonorrhea are similar to those of chlamydia: pelvic pain, painful or burning urination, vaginal discharge, drip from penis. It is spread to the mouth and throat as a result of oral sex with

a gonorrhea-infected partner, and to the rectum if the germ is transmitted during anal sex.

In women it infects the urethra, cervix, uterus, and tubes and can destroy the ability to have children. In men it can infect the urethra, prostate, and epididymis and can cause sterility.

Gonorrhea may cause heart trouble, skin disease, and joint problems in both men and women. It is sometimes fatal when left untreated. Like chlamydia, it may be transmitted to a baby at birth.

PID

"Since I started having sex about six months ago, I've been getting cramps all the time and fever and my periods are very heavy. I'm scared. Could this be VD?"

To make sure, go to a clinic or a gynecologist for a pelvic examination. These symptoms are associated with PID, or pelvic inflammatory disease, which is now common in the United States. It usually results from chlamydia, gonorrhea, or other bacterial infections that have gone untreated, allowing inflammation and abscess to develop in the lower abdomen. One out of every eight sexually active sixteen-year-old girls develops PID, and many become sterile because of it.

For most women, PID symptoms are fever and chills, lower abdominal pain, burning urination, painful intercourse, and heavy periods or irregular bleeding. But some women have mild symptoms or none at all.

PID has caused sterility in thousands of teenage girls in the United States.

Ectopic pregnancy is a common result of PID and requires surgery and hospitalization. If the condition is not diagnosed in time the outcome may be fatal.

HERPES

"I've heard of so many kids who have herpes. Is it all that easy to get?"
One of the most common viral diseases, herpes is easily transmitted during sexual acts. Today about twenty million people in the United States have herpes. These people periodically get blisters and sores on their lips or sex organs. Though not a life-threatening disease, it can be physically and emotionally painful, and there is no cure for it.

People with herpes may safely have sexual contact with partners during periods when they are free of symptoms. They are contagious only when blisters appear and just before their appearance, at which time they must avoid sexual contact. Those with herpes become familiar with the sensations—tingling, itching, or burning—that precede the appearance of the blisters.

You are more likely to contract herpes when your resistance is low or when you are very tired. Therefore, if you are sexually active, make sure that you get adequate rest.

One type of the herpes virus commonly causes cold sores on the lips. If you have a cold sore, avoid kissing until the sore has healed and disappeared. This strain of herpes is extremely contagious.

Avoid infecting an infant. It is important for a pregnant woman with herpes (or whose partner has herpes) to inform her physician of this fact at the beginning of the pregnancy. The doctor can then take precautions to insure the health of the baby.

VAGINITIS

"My vagina was itching and burning for a while. Finally, I went to a doctor. He said I have vaginitis. What does that mean?"
Vaginitis means inflammation of the vagina. It is a common condition—annoying, but not usually dangerous. Most women have a vaginitis experience sometime in their lives. There may be unusual discharge or burning or itching of vulva or vagina.

"Can my boyfriend get an STD from my vaginitis?"

Yes, men can get prostate and urethra infections from contact with a partner who has vaginitis. A woman may be infected by a man who, though free of symptoms, may be a carrier of a vaginitis-causing organism. Using condoms will prevent infection and reinfection.

NGU (Nongonococcal Urethritis)

"I thought I had the clap because I had a drip from my penis, but the doctor tested me and I have to take an antibiotic for NGU. What is that?"

Men who go to a doctor because of penis discharge are first tested for gonorrhea. If the test is negative, the diagnosis is NGU, which is short for nongonococcal urethritis. Urethritis means inflammation of the urethra. NGU is usually caused by chlamydia or bacteria. In men, it is at least twice as common as gonorrhea.

In women, a frequently occurring symptom of NGU is painful urination. NGU may cause damage to the reproductive organs.

SYPHILIS ("The siph" or "bad blood")

"I'm gay, and I have a sore on my lip, but it hardly hurts. Could this be a sign of AIDS?"

Only a doctor can diagnose it. A painless sore may be a sign of syphilis. Syphilis used to be considered the most dangerous of the sexually transmitted diseases. Nowadays it can be cured with antibiotics, but it is important to get the earliest possible treatment, since any damage that syphilis causes to the body is irreversible. If untreated, syphilis can cause heart disease, brain damage, blindness, and death.

Once a widespread disease, it is now much less common than either chlamydia or gonorrhea. Homosexual males account for about 50 percent of current cases.

A mother infected with syphilis can pass it on, through the

bloodstream, to her unborn child. The child may be born with birth defects, or develop serious medical problems soon after birth.

GENITAL WARTS (Venereal Warts)

Henry, a sixteen-year-old sophomore says:

"I have a couple of bumps on my penis that look something like tiny cauliflowers. They don't hurt, but I don't like the way they look. I haven't had sex in a few months but I wonder if I could have picked up VD from that girl."

Usually appearing on the sex organs or around the anus, these small, bumpy cauliflower-like warts show up from one to six months after sexual contact with an infected partner.

A woman may have a genital wart on her cervix and not be aware of it until a doctor calls it to her attention. Genital warts require medical treatment to keep them from spreading, enlarging, and infecting others.

CRABS (Pubic Lice)

Sybil, a suburban high school senior, was knowledgeable about layers of protection in her sexual relations, and she was fastidious about personal hygiene. Then something happened that she was not prepared for:

"I was itching in the genital area, and nothing helped. I tried creams and lotions and hot baths, but the itching only got worse. Finally, I went to the doctor, and he told me what I had. I almost fainted when he said I had crabs. How could I have an STD? Steve was my only boyfriend.

"The doctor gave me some medicine and told me to speak to my boyfriend, who might have crabs, too. It turned out that Steve didn't tell me because he didn't know what was bothering him, and he was sure it was just an itch that would go away. I felt like kicking myself.

"I had read in my textbook on STDs that contraceptive barriers didn't protect you from Crabs and Scabies—that you were supposed to have good light so that if your partner had a skin rash or anything suspicious, you would see it. With all our precautions, we had forgotten about light. It was more romantic to make love in the dark. Steve felt guilty, and I felt like a jerk."

These tiny parasites are spread through close physical contact or are sometimes picked up from bedding or shared clothing. They burrow under the skin, live in pubic hair, armpits, eyebrows, and chest hair. They can be treated with either medically prescribed or over-the-counter medication.

HEPATITIS B

This disease is a viral inflammation of the liver. It is usually transmitted either by contaminated needles or by intimate sexual contact, especially anal intercourse. The virus is present in body fluids: blood, semen, vaginal secretions, menstrual flow, saliva, and perspiration.

About two-thirds of hepatitis B infections produce no obvious symptoms. It is therefore unknowingly transmitted to sexual partners.

Symptoms that do occur are fatigue, loss of appetite, nausea, low-grade fever, diarrhea, and jaundice (yellowing of the skin, the eyes, and the mucous membranes). There is a risk of permanent liver damage and liver cancer. Most cases of hepatitis B are among males.

A successful vaccine has been developed for hepatitis B. However, once an infection occurs, there is no treatment other than rest and good nutrition.

"How do I avoid getting any of these diseases?"
The only sure way is to abstain from any form of sexual contact and from any drug use. You can keep your risk very low and still enjoy affection

and sensual experience by limiting your contacts to hugging, caressing, and the other ways of being loving described in Chapter Three.

If you are having sexual intercourse, the same precautions that you use to protect yourself from AIDS will protect you at the same time from most other STDs. They will also help to prevent unwanted pregnancies. Both partners should use contraceptives for double protection, each taking responsibility for maintaining his or her own health.

For the man there is the condom with a lubricant containing nonoxynol-9. For many young women the best choice is vaginal foam.

It is important to have a place, such as your own home, where you can wash your genitals before and after sexual contacts, and where you can urinate immediately afterwards. The automobile is not a safe and appropriate place for sex.

"Should I douche right after sex?"

No. It is better not to douche. Douching does nothing to prevent an STD infection and may even cause germs to go deeper into the cervical canal. Only the external genitals should be washed after sexual contacts.

There must be adequate light for you to be able to see each other's skin and genitals so that you can feel secure. If there are visible signs of STDs—rash, blisters, sores, or discharge—you need to hold off and talk to each other. People who are sightless need unhurried time for tactile exploration and candid talk.

If you are close enough to be sexually intimate, you are close enough to be able to talk over every aspect of your sexual experience. Ask about anything you want to know—past sexual experiences, contraception, STDs.

If you are troubled about any apparent risk, you have the choice of holding off or limiting your contacts to whatever sex play is risk-free.

"I've already had lots of partners. Does that put me in a high risk group?"

You can't change the past. Statistics show that the more sex partners a person has, the greater the likelihood of contracting or transmitting AIDS or other sexually transmitted diseases.

Long-time partners who are free of infection and restrict their sexual activity to each other can feel most secure. They face the least risk.

* * *

The same multiple barriers that protect us from most sexually transmitted diseases also help to prevent undesired conception. The next chapter discusses safety measures for coping with the problem of unplanned pregnancy.

9

When You're Not Ready for Pregnancy

"The kids say you can't get pregnant the first time. When should you start using birth control?"

Most young people who are planning to have sex say they want sex "to happen spontaneously." Almost all have sexual intercourse for the first time without any form of contraception. Many believe, mistakenly, that you don't get pregnant the first time you have intercourse. Others are willing to gamble by "taking a chance."

Ellen recalls her rude awakening:

"I don't know where I got the idea that you don't get pregnant the first time you do it. I guess from my friends—that's what they all said. So when Timmy and I were making out one night and he said, 'Let's do it,' I said, 'Okay!'

"I never thought I could be pregnant—even after I missed my period. But when it didn't come around the next month, I got really scared. When I told Timmy, he said, 'You can't be. We only did it once.'

"But he was very good and went to a clinic with me. That's where I found out I was pregnant—in my second month. Fourteen years old and pregnant! I wanted to go home and wake up from this awful dream. But this was one dream I couldn't wake up from. It was *real,* and I had some awful choices to make— decisions I wished someone else could make for me."

Today, people who have "spontaneous" unprotected sexual intercourse are not only betting against getting pregnant, but also against getting AIDS or other STDs. It is a deadly game, like playing Russian roulette with three bullets in the chamber.

In the Age of AIDS, spontaneity is a dangerous luxury. No one can afford to wait for sex "to happen spontaneously." Both intercourse and contraception must be *talked* about and *planned* for.

"What do you do if birth control is against your religion?"
If one or both partners has religious beliefs which forbid effective contraception, then intercourse must be postponed until marriage. This is a subject that should be discussed with your religious counselor.

Girls *can* and *do* get pregnant the very first time. Two out of five girls become pregnant during their teen years. Eighty-six percent of these girls have abortions to terminate the pregnancy. Therefore, the decision not to choose a contraceptive turns out, for most girls, to be a silent choice of abortion. Unless you have religious or other convictions forbidding it, abortion is one option.

A girl who has become pregnant has other options that are preferred by some religious counselors. She may choose to keep the baby and raise it alone or with the boy she loves. However, she should be aware that almost every boy who impregnates a girl outside of marriage eventually abandons her, whether or not they marry.

Giving the baby up for adoption is another option a pregnant girl may consider. There are a number of agencies and services to help a girl who chooses this option. Religious counselors can usually offer help along these lines.

This chapter opened with the question: **"When should you start using birth control?"** The answer depends partly on your religious convictions. For most young people, the answer is: **The very first time you have sexual intercourse, and every time thereafter, until you are mature enough to care for a family.** But if you are a member of a religious denomination that forbids premarital sexual contacts or birth control, you should discuss this question with your priest, minister, or rabbi.

"Does the pill protect me from AIDS?"

No, it does not. Nor does it protect you from herpes, from chlamydia, from genital warts, or from any of the other STDs that are so common today.

Unless this is your very first sexual contact and you are absolutely sure that this is your partner's very first contact, the present threat of AIDS and other STDs rules out the use of the pill, the IUD, sterilization, the rhythm and mucus method, douching, and of course, withdrawal. It also rules out, as contraceptive methods, anal sex and unprotected oral sex.

Safe Sex choices:

• Best of all, abstinence from sexual intercourse, and enjoying all the hugging and caressing that you like. (If your religious advisor believes that dating and caressing inevitably lead to sinful premarital intercourse, this view must be taken into serious consideration.)

• If abstinence is not acceptable to you, the remaining option is to use "layers of protection." The three safest choices are

1. Condom+ nonoxynol-9 lubricant + vaginal foam
2. Condom+ nonoxynol-9 lubricant + contraceptive sponge
3. Condom+ nonoxynol-9 lubricant + diaphragm+ gel or cream

"I read that all you need for safe sex is a condom and that the girl should buy them."

The girl who hands her partner a condom and thinks that her responsibility has ended is not adequately protecting herself from an unplanned pregnancy or the frightening results of a sexually transmitted infection.

Young women today who choose sexual intercourse must provide their own barrier contraceptive. Then, if there should be a condom accident, the woman's spermicidal barrier gives her significant protection—and protects the partner as well.

"But if we want to have a baby—then we can't use a condom. What should we do about STDs?"

Before you do anything else, go to your nearest Planned Parenthood Center or other sex information center (see page 115) for medical exams, prenatal counsel and care—so that your baby can be born healthy.

You will find your local Health Department listed in the phone book. The toll-free National STD Hotline (1-800-227-8922) will refer you to health-care providers in your area and will answer your questions.

"How can we remember all of this Safe Sex information?"

The next chapter boils it down to four simple rules.

10

Four Rules
for Safe Sex

There are four simple rules to follow for safe sex:

1. **Do not mix sex with alcohol or other drugs.** Both affect your judgment, causing you to take dangerous risks. And do not accept as a sexual partner someone who has been using alcohol or other drugs.

2. **Always insist on Safe Sex—or no sex.** Never give in to a partner's desire for unprotected sex just to please or to try to start a relationship or to attempt to save one.

   You can always suggest a safer alternative like dancing, or massage, or lovemaking without intercourse.

3. **If there is the slightest possibility that you may have sexual intercourse, make sure that you have condoms and foam with you.** Try them out when alone, so that you will know how to use them if you need to.

   If you are on the pill, you must still carry condoms or foam for protection against AIDS and other STDs.

4. Learn all you can about sexuality and Safe Sex right now.
Do not put off your self-education for that moment in the
future when you are overwhelmed by passion or persuasion.

The library is a fine place to start. If there is a YA (Young Adult)
Room you are fortunate. Otherwise, you will find your information in
the adult library. Besides those books on display, the "sex instruction
for youth" books are shelved by classification number.

Most sex instruction books are numbered 305.23, 306.7,
306.7088, 612.6, 612.661, 613.0433, 613.95, 613.953, or 613.955.
Most books about STDs are numbered 616.95. Most books about
AIDS are numbered 616.9792.

Become at home with the library's resources. Information that is
presented responsibly will help you to become comfortable with your
own sexual interests and choices and those of other people whose
interests and beliefs are very different from yours.

Then you may find that *you* have become a source of reliable sex
information for other young people.

* * *

In this Age of AIDS, what is most important to us all, and
especially to young people, is up-to-date information that dispels fear
and anxiety, eliminates hysteria and the tendency to blame victims of
the disease, and instead enables us to look forward optimistically to a
lifetime of fulfillment.

Where to Get Help
and Information

Everyone needs help from time to time. Sometimes it is difficult to ask for advice: sometimes it is even harder to find the assistance we need. National and public service organizations have been set up to assist young people when they need help and to offer it in a friendly way.

There are national toll-free hotlines, and community hotlines in some of the larger cities, providing information and referrals on sexuality and on other teen concerns. If you live in a small town or rural area, you may feel isolated. But sex information may be as close as your telephone. The 800 numbers are all toll-free.

AIDS: For information, call 1-800-342-AIDS. A twenty-four-hour seven day service is provided by the Centers for Disease Control. Any AIDS-related question will be answered clearly and responsibly.

For information about Alternative Test Sites in your area, where testing for the AIDS virus is available with pre-test and post-test counseling, call your city or state Board of Health. You will find it listed at the front of the phone book. In most states anonymity and confidentiality are guaranteed.

A special hotline for teens is 1-800-234-TEEN. Information on Safe Sex and AIDS is provided by teens, Monday through Friday, 5 P.M. to 9 P.M., Eastern Daylight Time.

STDs: For information, call 1-800-227-8922 (outside California) or 1-800-982-5883 (in California). This hotline is maintained by the American Social Health Association to provide counseling and also referrals to health care providers in your area.

Alcohol and other drugs: The New York State Council on Alcoholism offers information; call 1-800-252-2557. Alcoholics Anonymous is listed in most local phone books. The Drug Abuse Information Hotline number is 1-800-522-5353.

Contraception and pregnancy: Planned Parenthood is a national organization with chapters in many cities; listings will be found in local phone books. Planned Parenthood chapters provide sex-related medical, educational, counseling, and referral services, especially about contraception, pregnancy, and STDs.

Abortion: For abortion referral, call the National Abortion Federation Hotline, 1-800-772-9100. Or look up the Clergy Consultation Service on Abortion, or the local Department of Health, or Planned Parenthood—all listed in the phone book.

Alternatives to abortion: For counseling on alternatives, check your phone book for the Florence Crittendon Association or for your local Right to Life phone number.

Sex information: SIECUS (Sex Information and Education Council of the United States) provides information and referrals: 1-212-673-3850, Monday through Thursday, 1 P.M. to 8 P.M.; Friday 9 A.M. to 1 P.M.

The Los Angeles Sex Information Hotline provides information and referrals, nationally: 1-213-653-1123.

Sexual violence, date rape: New York Women Against Rape maintains a twenty-four-hour victim's service hotline: 1-212-577-7777, which provides counseling for young men and women. They will refer you to appropriate services in your area.

Words and Meanings

abortion—premature ending of a pregnancy, medically induced or spontaneous (miscarriage).

abstinence—refraining from having sexual intercourse.

acne—a pimply skin condition common in the teen years.

acquaintance rape—sexual relations forced on a person by someone the victim knows; a type of criminal assault.

acquired immune deficiency syndrome—AIDS.

adolescence—the teen years.

AIDS—acquired immune deficiency syndrome; a condition resulting from infection by HIV—the human immunodeficiency virus, which weakens the body's defenses, leaving the person susceptible to deadly forms of infection.

anal intercourse—insertion of penis into partner's rectum for sexual pleasure.

anal sex—stimulation, by any means, of the anus, rectum, or prostate, for sexual pleasure.

antibody—part of immune system; a blood particle that neutralizes any foreign body in the bloodstream.

anus—the body opening used for emptying bowels; "ass-hole."

areola—the dark ring around the nipple.

bacteria—microscopic plantlike organisms; some bacteria cause infection and others are harmless or helpful.

birth control—contraception; limiting the number of children born, especially by preventing conception.

bisexual—sexually active with both sexes.

boner—(slang) an erection; "hard-on."

Candidiasis—an infection, usually in the mouth or throat, caused by a yeast organism; thrush.

cervix—lower tip of the uterus, extending into and opening into the vagina.

chancre—painless, contagious sore on the mouth or genitals, usually caused by syphilis.

chlamydia—the most common sexually transmitted disease; its symptoms resemble those of gonorrhea.

circumcision—surgical removal of loose skin (foreskin) covering the head of the penis.

climax—orgasm, or "coming"; the high point of sexual excitement and muscle tension, usually very pleasurable; muscle spasms occur in the vagina, anus, male sex organs: in the male, there is usually an ejaculation of semen.

clitoral hood—tissue that covers the clitoris, especially when a woman is highly aroused.

clitoris—the small, sensitive female sex organ just above the urethra, not always visible; "clit."

coitus—penis-in-vagina sexual intercourse; fucking.

"come"—(slang) to have an orgasm or climax, to ejaculate; also used as noun, meaning semen; "cum."

conception—uniting of a male's sperm cell with a female's egg cell.

condom—"rubber"; a thin latex (or animal tissue) covering that is unrolled onto the penis before sexual intercourse to prevent STDs or unwanted pregnancy.

contraceptive—any device or agent used to prevent pregnancy.

contraceptive foam—a latherlike spermicide that is inserted in the vagina before sexual intercourse; when used with the condom, it prevents pregnancy and most STDs.

contraceptive sponge—a small, soft plastic sponge containing spermicide; it is inserted in the vagina against the cervix to prevent pregnancy and some STDs; best used with the condom.

crabs—(slang) pubic lice; tiny crablike parasites that burrow under the skin in hairy parts of the body.

cum—(slang) fluid ejaculated from penis; semen.

cunnilingus—licking the female genitals; oral sex.

cunt—(slang) vagina and vulva.

date rape—sex relations forced on people by their "dates"; a form of criminal assault.

diaphragm—a soft latex bowl-shaped contraceptive device inserted in the vagina against the cervix; it is used with spermicidal gel or cream; does not prevent all STDs.

douching—flushing the vagina (or rectum) with a liquid; never an effective method of contraception or STD prevention.

ejaculation—spurting of semen, a whitish fluid that contains sperm, from the penis, almost always accompanying male orgasm; with consecutive repeated sex acts, a male may experience dry orgasm.

117

erotic—having to do with sexual expression.

erection—swelling and stiffening of penis, usually caused by sexual excitement; "hard-on," "boner."

estrogen—a hormone (chemical produced by glands in the body) that causes development of female sexual characteristics, the rapid changes of early teens; contained in "combination" contraceptive pill.

fallopian tube—one of two narrow tubes in the female in which the egg travels from an ovary to the uterus.

fellatio—sucking the penis; "giving head"; "blow job"; "frenching."

fertile—capable of getting pregnant.

fertilization—joining of male's sperm and female's egg, usually in the fallopian tube.

foam—a vaginal contraceptive (*see* contraceptive foam), sold without prescription.

foreplay—petting, when followed by sexual intercourse.

foreskin—the fold of skin covering the tip of the penis; usually removed by circumcision.

fuck—to insert penis in vagina, usually with rhythmic thrusting; for some, including many gay men, to insert in rectum with thrusting; sexual intercourse; to "have sex."

gay—homosexual; usually referring to male.

gender—male or female.

genital herpes—a sexually transmitted disease causing blisters around the genitals.

genitals—the external sex organs.

glans—the head of the penis or of the clitoris.

gonorrhea—a sexually transmitted disease caused by a bacterial infection; sometimes without symptoms, males may have pus discharge from penis; "clap," "drip."

growth spurt—a period, usually in early teens, of rapid increase in height.

gynecologist—a doctor who specializes in the health problems of women's reproductive systems.

hard-on—(slang) a stiffening of the penis; erection, "boner."

hepatitis—a liver infection, sometimes sexually transmitted.

heterosexual—a person who is most attracted to people of the other sex.

HIV—human immunodeficiency virus; the name that is in current use for the virus that causes AIDS.

homophobia—fear and hatred of homosexuals; a common emotional disturbance.

homosexual—a person who is most attracted to people of the same sex.

hormones—chemicals that glands produce; they cause the body and emotion changes of the early teen years.

horny—(slang) feeling sexy; sexually aroused.

hymen—thin tissue (mucous membrane) that partly closes the entrance to the vagina in most girls who have not had sexual intercourse or have not torn or stretched it in exercise or sport.

immune system—the body's system of defense against foreign objects (such as germs or organ transplants) that enter the body.

incest—sexual relations between close relatives.

intercourse—*see* sexual intercourse.

IUD—intrauterine device; an object, usually made of plastic, inserted in the uterus by a doctor or nurse to prevent pregnancy; no longer recommended.

IV drugs—intravenous drugs; heroin, amphetamines, or other chemicals injected into veins.

jackoff—(slang) masturbate; "jerkoff."

labia—the female genital lips around the vaginal opening.

lesbian—a woman who prefers another woman as lover; homosexual woman.

masturbation—stimulating the sex organs for pleasurable feelings; "jacking off," "playing with oneself."

menstruation—monthly shedding of blood and tissue that make up the uterus lining; "period."

miscarriage—expelling of fetus between the third and seventh month.

morning-after pill—an unsafe form of contraception; doctor-prescribed hormone pill taken after unprotected intercourse.

necking—caressing and kissing, above-the-waist petting.

NGU—nongonococcal urethritis; an inflammation of the urethra, usually caused by chlamydia.

nocturnal emission—wet dream; ejaculation of semen in sleep or on waking; experienced by most males.

opportunistic infection—an illness that develops in a person with a weakened immune system.

oral sex—mouth-to-penis or mouth-to-vagina sexual contact; cunnilingus or fellatio.

orgasm—the pleasurable climax that results from a buildup of sexual excitement, marked by muscle spasms followed by release of tension; in males, usually accompanied by ejaculation; "coming."

ovaries—two glands that contain egg cells and produce female hormones.

penis—male sex organ, used also for urination; "cock."

petting—caressing the whole body, usually including the sex organs, sometimes to orgasm; "fooling around."

PID—pelvic inflammatory disease; a serious disease of the fallopian tubes and adjacent region, usually caused by chlamydia infection.

Pneumocystis carinii pneumonia—a formerly rare disease that attacks AIDS patients.

poppers—(slang) drugs inhaled during sexual activity; amyl nitrite, associated with AIDS.

prostate gland—a part of the male reproductive system within the body, producing a part of the semen; sensitive to stimulation.

prostitute—a person who exchanges sexual acts for money; "hooker."

rape—sexual assault; forced sexual intercourse.

rectum—lower end of the digestive tract, just inside the anus.

rubber—(slang) condom, a latex bag that fits on the penis; protects against the transmission of disease and against unwanted pregnancy.

scabies—skin irritation and itching caused by tiny insects (mites) that burrow into the skin; usually on the external sex organs and hands.

scrotum—the sac containing the testicles; "bag."

semen—whitish sticky fluid that spurts from the penis during orgasm; "cum."

sexual intercourse—sexual play with penis in vagina, usually accompanied by rhythmic pelvic movement; "having sex."

sodomy—usually means some form of sexual intercourse other than penis-in-vagina; sometimes used to mean sexual contacts with animals, sometimes oral or anal intercourse, sometimes homosexual contacts.

sperm—a reproductive cell in semen; when it joins an egg cell in a woman's body, she becomes pregnant.

spermicide—a substance that can kill sperm in order to prevent pregnancy; chemical contraceptive.

sponge—*see* contraceptive sponge.

STD—sexually transmitted disease; one of many diseases that are usually spread from person to person during sexual contacts; formerly called VD.

syndrome—a group of symptoms and signs that together are characteristic of a disease.

syphilis—a serious sexually transmitted disease; easily treated, though many fail to seek treatment; "the syph."

testicles—two egg-shaped glands in the scrotum; "balls."

trichomoniasis—a common sexually transmitted disease; some carriers have no symptoms; the most common symptom is a foul-smelling vaginal discharge; "trich."

urethra—the tube through which urine is passed; in the male it has two uses: for urine and for ejaculation of semen.

uterus—female reproductive organ (at the end of the vagina) in which an unborn baby develops; womb.

vagina—the soft, elastic muscular passageway between the uterus and the external sex organs (labia and clitoris); cunt.

VD—venereal disease; gonorrhea and syphilis; now called sexually transmitted disease (STD).

virgin—a person who has never had intercourse.

vulva—the female external sex organs; large and small labia, clitoris, and mons; cunt.

wet dream—ejaculation during sleep; nocturnal emission.

Some Helpful Books for Young People

AIDS

Hyde, Margaret O., and Elizabeth H. Forsyth. *AIDS: What Does It Mean to You?* New York: Walker, 1986.

Kesden, Bradley, and Oralee Wachter. *Sex, Drugs and AIDS*. New York: Bantam, 1987.

Langone, John. *AIDS: The Facts*. Boston: Little, Brown, 1988.

Madaras, Lynda. *Lynda Madaras Talks to Teens About AIDS*. New York: Newmarket, 1988.

Silverstein, Alvin, and Virginia B. Silverstein. *AIDS: Deadly Threat*. Hillside, NJ: Enslow, 1986.

Alcohol and Other Drugs

Berger, Gilda. *Making Up Your Mind About Drugs*. New York: Lodestar Books, 1988.

Coffey, Wayne R. *Straight Talk About Drinking*. New York: NAL, 1988.

Coffey, Wayne R., and Eric Ryerson. *When Your Parents Drink Too Much: A Book for Teenagers*. New York: Random House, 1985.

Graeber, Laurel. *Are You Dying for a Drink? Teenagers and Alcohol Abuse*. New York: Messner, 1985.

Hyde, Margaret O. *Alcohol: Uses and Abuses*. Hillside, NJ: Enslow, 1988.

Jussim, Daniel. *Drug Tests and Polygraphs: Tools or Violations of Privacy?* New York: Messner, 1988.

Madison, Arnold. *Drugs and You*. Rev. ed. New York: Messner, 1984.

Newman, Susan. *It Won't Happen to Me*. New York: Perigee Press, 1987.

Washton, Arnold M., and Donna Boundy. *Cocaine and Crack: What You Need to Know*. Hillside, NJ: Enslow, 1989.

Assertiveness

McFarland, Rhoda. *Coping Through Assertiveness*. New York: Rosen, 1986.

Contraception

Balis, Andrea. *What Are You Using?* New York: Dial, 1981.

Everett, Jane, and Walter D. Glanze. *The Condom Book.* New York: Signet, 1987.

Lieberman, E. James, and Ellen Peck. *Sex and Birth Control, A Guide for the Young.* Rev. ed. New York: Harper and Row, 1981.

Dating

Butler, John. *Christian Ways to Date, Go Steady, and Break Up.* Cincinnati: Standard, 1978.

McCoy, Kathy. *The Teenage Body Book Guide to Dating.* New York: Simon and Schuster, 1983.

Reichert, Richard. *Sexuality and Dating: A Christian Perspective.* Winona, MI: St. Mary's Press, Christian Bros., 1981.

Early Teens

Betancourt, Jeanne. *Am I Normal?* New York: Avon, 1983.

———. *Dear Diary.* New York: Avon, 1983.

Madaras, Lynda, with Area Madaras. *What's Happening to My Body? Book for Girls.* New York: Newmarket, 1983.

Madaras, Lynda, with Dane Saavedra. *What's Happening to My Body? Book for Boys.* New York: Newmarket, 1984.

McCoy, Kathy. *The Teenage Body Book.* Rev. ed. New York: Simon and Schuster, 1987.

Homosexuality

Hanckel, Frances, and John Cunningham. *A Way of Love, a Way of Life: A Young Person's Introduction to What It Means to Be Gay.* New York: Lothrop, Lee, and Shepard, 1979.

Heron, Ann, ed. *One Teenager in Ten.* Boston: Alyson, 1985.

Landau, Elaine. *Different Drummer: Homosexuality in America.* New York: Julian Messner, 1986.

Menstruation

Gardner-Loulan, JoAnn, Bonnie Lopez, and Marcia Quackenbush. *Period.* Rev. ed. San Francisco: Volcano, 1981.

Rape

Bode, Janet. *Rape.* New York: Franklin Watts, 1979.

Safe Sex

McIlvenna, Ted, ed. *The Complete Guide to Safe Sex.* San Francisco: Specific Press, 1987.

Sexuality

Bell, Ruth, et al. *Changing Bodies, Changing Lives.* New York: Rev. ed. Random House, 1988.

Comfort, Alex, and Jane Comfort. *The Facts of Love.* New York: Crown, 1979.

Gittelsohn, Roland B. *Love, Sex, and Marriage: A Jewish View.* Rev. ed. New York: Union of American Hebrew Congregations, 1980.

Hamilton, Eleanor. *Sex With Love.* Boston: Beacon Press, 1978.

Johnson, Eric. *Love and Sex in Plain Language*, 4th ed. New York: Simon and Schuster, 1985.

Pomeroy, Wardell B. *Boys and Sex.* Rev. ed. New York: Dell, 1981.

———. *Girls and Sex.* Rev. ed. New York: Dell, 1981.

Voss, Jacqueline, and Jay Gale. *A Young Woman's Guide to Sex.* New York: Holt, 1986.

STDs

Landau, Elaine. *Sexually Transmitted Diseases.* Hillside, NJ: Enslow, 1986.

Lumiere, Richard, and Stephanie Cook. *Healthy Sex and Keeping It That Way.* New York: Simon and Schuster, 1983.

Index

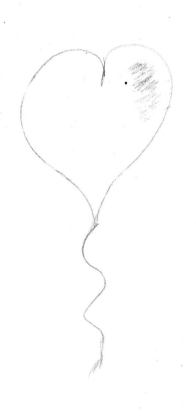